Writing Clearly for
Clients and Colleagues

Related books of interest

Writing Clearly for Clients and Colleagues

The Human Service Practitioner's Guide

Natalie Ames
North Carolina State University

Katy FitzGerald

LYCEUM
BOOKS, INC.

Chicago, IL 60637

© 2015 by Lyceum Books, Inc.

Published by

LYCEUM BOOKS, INC.
5758 S. Blackstone Avenue
Chicago, Illinois 60637
773-643-1903 fax
773-643-1902 phone
lyceum@lyceumbooks.com
www.lyceumbooks.com

6 5 4 3 2 1   14 15 16 17 18

ISBN 978-1-935871-65-1

Printed in the United States of America.

Library of Congress Cataloging-in-Publication Data

Ames, Natalie.
  Writing clearly for clients and colleagues : the human service practitioner's
guide / Natalie Ames, Katy FitzGerald.
      pages cm
  Includes bibliographical references and index.
  ISBN 978-1-935871-65-1
  1. Communication in social work. 2. Communication in human services.
3. Written communication. 4. Social service—Authorship. 5. Human
services—Authorship. I. FitzGerald, Katy. II. Title.
  HV29.7.A44   2015
  808.06′6361—dc23
                                                        2014016923

Contents

Figures, Tables, Examples, and Exercises

FIGURES

TABLES

EXAMPLES

EXERCISES

Introduction

WHY WE WROTE THIS BOOK

Although writing may not be part of your job description, or a task you love, writing is a necessary skill for most human service professionals, but the ability to write clearly and concisely does not come naturally to many of us. We hope this book will motivate you to think about how you write and to take action to make your agency's written materials easier for your clients—and others—to understand.

The main focus of this book is on how to create readable materials for clients with limited literacy skills, but it covers much more than that. Once you develop the skills to write in ways your clients can understand, you can use the same skills to make everything you write easier to read. If you have ever waded through a convoluted memo, a rambling case summary, an overly detailed program description, or a poorly organized training manual, you know how important it is for written materials to state clearly and concisely what readers need to know. Whether your audience is made up of colleagues, team members, volunteers, donors, legislators, agency administrators, or the general public, the less time and effort it takes for them to understand your message, the more likely they are to read it.

The electronic age has introduced new possibilities for communicating with clients, colleagues, volunteers, donors, and the public. Nearly all of us use email on a daily basis. Most agencies have a website that provides infor-mation to the public. Some agencies post application forms online. Others have Facebook pages and Twitter feeds. Clarity and conciseness are just as important for these electronic forms of communication as they are for written words printed on paper. This book shows you how to apply the principles of readability to your electronic communications in order to get your intended messages across.

WHAT YOU WILL FIND IN THIS BOOK

Chapter 1 explains the multiple definitions of literacy and how those definitions apply to clients likely to seek services from human service agencies. It describes the effects of limited literacy skills on clients' capacity to understand and make use of printed information as well as their ability to fill out applications and forms. The chapter provides explicit guidelines for improving the readability of all the printed materials human service agencies provide to clients.

Chapter 2 introduces two principles central to creating readable materials: plain language and active voice. Examples throughout the chapter illustrate how plain language and active voice improve readability. It includes an exercise on using plain language and examples that illustrate the differences between active and passive voice. The chapter includes a list of plain language words that can replace the "fancy" words human service agencies commonly use in their publications.

In chapter 3 you will find instructions and techniques for revising existing materials and developing new, readable materials for individuals with limited literacy skills. It includes examples and checklists to help you identify your target audiences and develop messages that target specific audiences with relevant, culturally appropriate information.

In chapter 4 you will learn the technical aspects of developing and revising easy-to-read materials, including instructions for measuring reading grade levels. The section on overall appropriateness explains the many factors, besides reading grade level, that can limit or improve poor readers' ability to comprehend print materials. It includes information about choosing and incorporating illustrations as well as recommendations, examples, and checklists for evaluating features that are critical for achieving readability.

Chapter 5 offers detailed instructions and materials you can use to determine if your target audience can read and understand the materials you design for them. It also provides suggestions for using feedback from your target audience to make revisions that will improve readability.

Chapter 6 connects the concept of readability to the written materials human service agencies provide to audiences other than clients. Examples throughout the chapter demonstrate how to apply the guidelines for readability to improve agency communications with board members, donors, funders, volunteers, and the media. The chapter also includes suggestions for communicating more clearly within your agency.

Chapter 7 applies readability guidelines to human service agencies' use of electronic communications such as email, texting, and social media. It includes suggestions for the content and layout of websites and illustrates how improving readability can make websites more informative, accessible, and valuable to a wide range of audiences.

Chapter 8 connects the concept of readability with the skills human service professionals need in order to write good documentation. The chapter offers specific guidelines for documentation and a series of exercises that enable readers to practice applying the guidelines.

We have also provided an appendix with a review of the basics of grammar and punctuation, which are the foundation for good professional writing. It explains and illustrates common errors and provides exercises that enable you to practice correct usage. Even if you don't share our fascination with grammatical correctness, we hope you will find this information useful, and possibly even interesting, as a reference.

This book is designed to help you to write simply and clearly no matter who your audience is. Our primary goal is to teach human service professionals how to write clearly enough to communicate with clients with limited literacy skills. Once you learn to do that, you can apply those techniques to improve all of your professional writing. Whether you are writing a brochure, sending an email, documenting in a case record, or creating content for an agency website, we will show you how to make your messages clear and easy to understand.

Why Readability Matters

Most people choose to read and to keep reading only when they believe there will be some benefit in doing so and only when they cannot get the same information in easier ways.

—**K. A. Shriver,** *Dynamics in Document Design*

For people with limited literacy skills, reading is not an easy way to get information. Those of us who take the ability to read for granted cannot truly comprehend just how difficult reading is for those individuals. To give you a personal understanding of how difficult it can be for a person with limited literacy skills to attempt to read, read the paragraph in figure 1.1.

Figure 1.1   **Nac Ouy Daer Siht Hpargarap?**

Fi uoy dnatsrednu woh tluciffid ti si rof elpoep htiw detimil ycaretil slliks ot daer, uoy lliw wonk yhw ti si os tnatropmi ot ekam erus ruoy s'ycnega tnirp slairetam era ysae ot daer. Peek ni dnim woh tluciffid ti saw ot daer siht eht txen emit uoy era elbisnopser rof gnitirw gnihtemos taht ruoy ycnega lliw evig ot stneilc. Si ti elbissop taht ruoy ycnega nac yfilpmis sti tnirp slairetam ot ekam meht erom elbadaer? Fi os, siht koob lliw pleh uoy hguorht taht ssecorp.

The paragraph was, of course, written backward. Without being able to recognize or sound out the words in the paragraph, how did you go about trying to read it? If you tried to decipher each word, you undoubtedly understood the meaning of individual words, but the effort of deciphering them probably compromised your ability to combine those words into a meaningful whole.

1

Thus, even if you read all the words, you may not comprehend the message in the paragraph. Perhaps you got frustrated and gave up before you reached the end. Whatever your reaction, the purpose of this brief exercise is to make real for you how difficult it is for people with limited literacy skills to read and understand printed words. They cannot skim through a sentence, let alone a paragraph, to grasp its meaning. If they are faced with a lot of print, they often give up without even trying to finish. (If you gave up before finishing, see figure 1.2 at the end of the chapter for a translation.)

It is important to distinguish between the academic writing you did in school and the professional writing that will get your messages across as a human service professional. Standard college and graduate school writing assignments, such as research papers and literature reviews, are not the best preparation for professional writing. The goal of professional writing should be to identify the information a specific audience needs to know and give them that information clearly, simply, and concisely. Too often, the academic writing that earns good grades consists of long words incorporated into enough complex sentences to fill a specified number of pages. That kind of writing will discourage clients from reading the content of your agency's materials even if the information might be valuable to them.

This may be the electronic age, but human service agencies still use the written word, whether on paper or on websites, to provide information to a variety of audiences. Unfortunately, most agency materials are not written clearly and simply enough for people with limited literacy skills to understand (King, Winton, & Adkins, 2003; Mavrogenes, Hanson, & Winkley, 1977; Wilson, Wallace, & DeVoe, 2009; Yick, 2008). Giving your clients pamphlets, flyers, booklets, application forms, or other printed materials that they cannot readily understand is a waste of the time, effort, and expense invested in producing those materials.

If you work for a human service agency, you probably distribute a great deal of printed material. Do you ask clients to complete applications for service? Does your agency provide brochures, booklets, flyers, and/or fact sheets to inform prospective clients and the community about its programs and services? Do you use printed materials to educate clients and community members about social problems and issues related to your agency's mission? Perhaps you give clients written rules, regulations, or eligibility criteria. If you are like most human service professionals who use print to provide critical information, you may not be aware of the factors that influence whether your intended audiences can comprehend the messages you are trying to convey. What you need to know is that it is possible to use print to communicate with clients who have limited literacy skills *if* you know how to make those materials readable.

We firmly believe that it is not our clients' responsibility to try to understand what we are attempting to communicate. It is our responsibility to make our communications as clear and understandable as possible. We want to emphasize that writing clearly and simply is NOT what some people refer to as "dumbing down" the materials. When you give clients information they can understand in the form of easy-to-read print materials, you are respecting their needs and abilities. This is consistent with the ethical values of the human service professions, including:

- the National Association of Social Workers *Code of Ethics* principle of "respect[ing] the inherent dignity and worth of the person (NASW, 2008, p. 5)
- the *Ethical Standards for Human Service Professionals* requirement that clients be treated "with respect, acceptance and dignity" (National Organization for Human Services, 2009, n.p.)
- the American Counseling Association *Code of Ethics* mandate to "encourage client growth and development in ways that foster the interest and welfare of clients" (American Counseling Association, 2005, p. 4)

CONNECTING THE DOTS BETWEEN POVERTY, EDUCATIONAL ATTAINMENT, AND READING ABILITY

The less education people have, the more likely they are to have limited literacy skills (Corley, 2003; White & Dillow, 2005). Low educational attainment and limited literacy skills generally prevent people from qualifying for jobs that pay well, thus they are more likely to be poor than those who are better educated. An estimated 22 percent of American adults have minimal literacy skills, meaning they read at or below the fifth grade level. This group includes immigrants as well as people with visual, physical, mental, and psychological impairments (Kutner, Greenberg, Jin, & Paulsen, 2006). Of those with the lowest literacy skills, 43 percent live in poverty, 17 percent receive food stamps, and 70 percent do not have full- or part-time jobs. Adults with low literacy levels are more likely to be homeless or unemployed or to hold very low paying jobs (Kutner et al., 2006).

The results of the 2003 National Assessment of Adult Literacy (NAAL) illustrate the relationships among poverty, low educational attainment, and limited literacy (Kutner et al., 2006). Estimates based on NAAL findings indicate that 47 percent of adult welfare recipients did not graduate from high school and that approximately 70 percent of these individuals have limited literacy skills. Many of these people end up as the clients of human service agencies. Individuals with limited literacy skills can understand simply written materials but will have difficulty drawing any conclusions beyond what the words clearly state (Sabatini, Sawaki, Shore, & Scarborough, 2010).

Most human service practitioners are aware that some of the clients who seek their services have difficulty with reading. We should note, however, that it is not only poor people or those with low educational attainment who can benefit when you provide easy-to-read materials. Although people who are poor may be more apt to have difficulty with reading, a significant number of Americans are not skilled readers. The average reading level for American adults is ninth grade (Kutner et al., 2006). According to the US Census Bureau (2006–2008), approximately 15.5 percent of American adults age 25 and older did not graduate from high school and 29.6 percent have only a high school diploma or general equivalency diploma (GED). However, the highest grade a person completed in school does not necessarily tell us how well they can read. There is evidence that many individuals read four to five grade levels below the highest grade they report having completed in school (Arnold et al., 2006; Doak, Doak, & Root, 1996; National Work Group on Literacy and Health, 1998). This means that many individuals, even if they completed the twelfth grade, read at only a seventh or eighth grade level. Rather than putting the burden of comprehension on our clients, we believe that this reality makes us, as human service professionals, responsible for providing them with easy-to-read print materials.

What is the significance of the statistics on Americans' reading ability? If your agency serves clients who are poor, it undoubtedly serves clients with limited literacy skills; thus the readability of your print materials is critical. Be aware, however, that people from all walks of life may have difficulty reading complex materials no matter their age, educational background, financial status, or ethnicity.

Your clients are the audience that will benefit most if you improve the readability of your agency's print materials. We wish to stress, however, that other audiences with whom your agency communicates may also appreciate receiving print materials that are easy to read. The volunteers, funders, legislators, community members, and/or donors with whom your agency communicates about its programs and services are busy people who have many demands on their time. They are more likely to read a short piece with a clearly stated message targeted to their interests.

HOW LITERACY IS DEFINED

Many people define literacy as simply the ability to read and write. That is the definition of literacy you will find in the dictionary. However, current definitions of literacy extend beyond the ability to read and write. The 2003 NAAL defines literacy as "the ability to use printed and written information to function in society, to achieve one's goals, and to develop one's knowledge and potential" (White & Dillow, 2005, p. 4). The NAAL is significant because it offers the most comprehensive statistics available on adult literacy in the United States. It surveyed 19,714 adults (defined as age 16 and older) from all fifty states and the District of Columbia, defining and measuring three components of literacy: prose, document, and quantitative.

Prose literacy includes the knowledge and skills people need to find, understand, and make use of information that is organized in paragraphs. Individuals must have prose literacy skills to understand the content of pamphlets, brochures, booklets, and educational materials written in a narrative style. The NAAL measured participants' literacy skills by having them complete a variety of tasks. It defined four levels of prose literacy skills:

- Below Basic—adults who have only very simple and concrete literacy skills, ranging from being nonliterate in English to having the ability to locate easily identifiable information in short, simple printed materials
- Basic—adults who can carry out simple, everyday literacy activities
- Intermediate—adults capable of moderately challenging literacy activities
- Proficient—adults who can perform complex, challenging literacy activities

NAAL findings have implications for any human service agency that serves diverse populations. Forty-three percent of all survey participants had prose literacy skills that fell into the *below basic* or *basic* literacy categories. Twenty-four percent of African American and 44 percent of Hispanic survey participants scored at the below basic level (Kutner, Greenberg, & Baer, 2005). Fifty-eight percent of participants with incomes below the poverty level had below basic skills even though they made up only 17 percent of the sample (White & Dillow, 2005). Clients with poor prose literacy skills will have difficulty finding specific information in a brochure or booklet. They may not understand how the information applies to them or what it is instructing them to do.

Document literacy involves the knowledge and skills people need to find, understand, and make use of information that is arranged in columns, rows, and cells rather than in paragraphs. Educated people are usually accustomed to locating information that is laid out in these nonnarrative formats. Clients with poor document literacy skills will have difficulty comprehending applications and forms, figuring out schedules, or making sense of a chart containing information about various programs an agency offers.

Although prose literacy and document literacy are the most pertinent for human service agency clients, poor quantitative literacy puts people at an additional disadvantage. *Quantitative literacy* is the ability to add, subtract, multiply, and divide. These are the skills needed to balance a checkbook or to use an order form to buy something. These skills are also necessary to complete forms that require adding various sources of household income to come up with a total. Clients with poor prose and document literacy skills will have difficulty reading the instructions and correctly filling out application forms for various kinds of assistance. Poor quantitative literacy skills further compromise their ability to complete the forms.

WHAT YOU NEED TO KNOW ABOUT READING AND COMPREHENSION

Reading research provides insight into the difficulties adults with limited literacy skills experience. It may be helpful to summarize briefly what the research tells us about the process of reading because this knowledge is the foundation for the readability guidelines we present later in this chapter.

In order to read fluently, people must have phonemic awareness, which is the ability to recognize and separate the sounds in words. They also need the vocabulary and language comprehension skills to understand what the words mean (Rapp, van den Broek, McMaster, Kendeou, & Espin, 2007; Sabatini et al., 2010).

Adults' ability to recognize words appears to play a role in comprehension. Good word recognition does not guarantee good comprehension, but it is an important element (Stanovich, 1996). Readers who cannot recognize words must decode them one word at a time. The more mental effort they have to invest in identifying individual words, the less likely they are to be able to connect the words they are reading into a meaningful whole (Mellard, Woods, & Fall, 2011). They may understand the individual words but miss the message the words are intended to convey.

Some research indicates that readers' prior knowledge about a topic may help them understand new information (Mellard & Fall, 2012; Rapp et al., 2007). Prior knowledge provides a foundation that can help people make sense of new information (Allington & McGill-Franzen, 2009). It is important to remember this when you give clients printed information. If the material you give them requires prior knowledge to be meaningful, they may not have the basis for understanding it. Be careful about assuming that any given piece of information is something "everyone knows."

Finally, listening comprehension appears to be related to reading comprehension. Listening comprehension is a person's ability to understand spoken language. Individuals who have difficulty understanding verbal communication may also have problems with reading comprehension (Daneman,

1996). While you would not want to assume that all clients who have trouble understanding what you tell them have limited literacy skills, it is worth remembering that there may be a connection between listening and reading skills.

GUIDELINES FOR CREATING READABLE MATERIALS

As we will discuss in chapter 2, plain language and active voice are the foundation for clear writing. Increasing readability for audiences with limited literacy skills, however, requires a great deal more than using plain language and active voice. The sixteen guidelines that follow are all important for creating readable written materials.

1. Do not use all capital letters.

In electronic communication, using capital or upper case letters is the equivalent of shouting. When you want to call attention to important information, you may be tempted to use capital letters to make it stand out. The problem is that capital letters are harder for anyone to read but are especially difficult for people with limited literacy skills. Because all capital letters are the same height, words written in capital letters have similar shapes. Lower case letters vary in shape and appearance: CAPITALS and capitals. The variations in the shapes of lower case letters give readers visual cues that make letters and words easier to decipher (Doak et al., 1996) as example 1.1 illustrates.

Example 1.1	Comparing ALL CAPS to Upper and Lower Case Letters
CAPITAL LETTERS ARE SIMILAR IN APPEARANCE WHICH MAKES WORDS HARD FOR POOR READERS TO DECIPHER. BECAUSE LOWER CASE LETTERS VARY A GREAT DEAL IN SHAPE, THEY OFFER MORE VISUAL CUES TO HELP READERS RECOGNIZE THEM.	Capital letters are similar in appearance, which makes words hard for poor readers to decipher. Because lower case letters vary a great deal in shape, they offer more visual cues to help readers recognize them.

2. Use ragged right margins instead of a justified right margin.

A justified right margin means that the ends of all the lines of type are perfectly even on the right side of the page. There is no doubt that justified right margins look polished and professional. If your primary concern is improving readability, however, you must put readability above appearance. This means using ragged right margins rather than justified right margins. In order to justify the right margin, the spacing between words and letters must be inconsistent, as you can see in example 1.2. This variable spacing makes following the text more difficult for any reader. It is especially problematic for poor readers who are trying to decipher the text word by word. The need for their eyes to constantly adjust to the spacing adds another barrier to comprehension.

Example 1.2

Comparing a Justified Right Margin to a Ragged Right Margin

Justified Right Margin

To improve readability, use ragged right margins rather than justified text. Justified text has even right margins. Agencies use it for their print materials because it looks more formal and professional than ragged right margins. However, it is more difficult to read because the eye must keep adjusting to different amounts of space between letters and words.

Ragged Right Margin

To improve readability, use ragged right margins rather than justified text. Justified text has even right margins. Agencies use it for their print materials because it looks more formal and professional than ragged right margins. However, it is more difficult to read because the eye must keep adjusting to different amounts of space between letters and words.

---

3. Use underline, boldface, or white space for emphasis.

We have explained why you should not use capital letters for emphasis. Underlining, boldface, or surrounding the text you want to emphasize with white space will make it jump out at the reader. Be careful, however, to emphasize only those points you really want to stand out. The purpose of underlining should be to call attention to specific information you want

<u>readers to notice. But, as you can see from this example, underlining a lot of text can be distracting and may discourage poor readers.</u> **You can see, too, that the same is true for boldface. Making extended passages bold can discourage people from reading the text. Using a great deal of boldface text is just as distracting as using a lot of underlining.**

Surrounding an important point with plenty of white space is the best way to draw the reader's eye.

4. Do not use unusual, decorative, or multiple fonts.

Word processing programs offer hundreds of fonts to choose from. It can be tempting to incorporate fancy, curly, or cursive fonts into a pamphlet or brochure to make some part of the text stand out. The reality is that many unusual fonts can be difficult for even fluent readers to decipher, and using them will discourage poor readers from trying. We include italics in this category because italicized letters can be hard to distinguish, which decreases the readability of text. Rather than italicizing for emphasis, underline or use boldface. You should also avoid using multiple fonts; one readable font, with perhaps a second for titles and headings, is ideal. As demonstrated in example 1.3, it takes more effort to read fancy print and multiple fonts.

Example 1.3	Fancy and Multiple Fonts

Do not use fancy fonts or italics. They make letters and words hard to decipher. They decrease poor readers' comprehension. Do not use multiple fonts in the same document. It looks messy. *It's also hard for the eyes to adjust to different fonts.* Using fancy or multiple fonts will confuse readers and decrease readability.

Serif type increases readability (Doak et al., 1996). Serif letters have small lines or projections at the top and bottom. Sans serif typefaces do not have these projections. Serif fonts are easier to read because they make the letters easier to differentiate. They also help guide the reader's eye from one letter to the next. You can see the difference in example 1.4. We prefer Times New Roman, which is the font most often recommended for readability. Other serif fonts include Garamond, Georgia, and Cambria.

Example 1.4   **Comparing Serif and Sans Serif Fonts**

This is an example of serif type. Notice the little lines at the tops and bottoms of the letters.

This is an example of sans serif type. There are no lines at the tops and bottoms of the letters.

---

5. Do not use very small type.

Do not use very small type. It discourages poor readers, and many older adults cannot see it. The first two sentences here are written in 8-point type. In case you could not read them, they say: Do not use very small type. It discourages poor readers, and many older adults cannot see it. This is 10-point type. It is larger than 8-point but still difficult for many people to read. This is 12-point type. You should use at least a 12-point font. This is 14-point type. You may want to use this for materials aimed at clients if you have enough space.

6. Do not center the text on a page or in a column.

You may like the way centered text looks. However, as you can see, it is distracting when the lines of print begin and end in different places. Centered text is especially hard for people with limited literacy skills to follow because it interrupts the flow of the print when the eye must adjust to different starting and ending places for each line.

7. Define terms or give examples.

As we noted earlier, research indicates that both vocabulary and prior knowledge play a role in reading comprehension. Much of the information human service agencies provide to clients contains vocabulary that may be unfamiliar to clients. It is also possible that some or all of the information in agency publications may not relate to your audience's prior knowledge. We realize that even if you use plain language, you cannot always avoid all terms that clients might not understand. What you can do is to define such terms in plain language or give examples so that the reader knows what the terms mean, as illustrated in example 1.5.

| Example 1.5 | Two Examples of Defining and Explaining Terms |

When we must remove children from the home, we attempt to place them with resource families. Resource families are relatives, foster parents, or adoptive parents who live close to the children's home.

Our program helps at-risk teens. At-risk teens are teens who may be having problems at school, at home, or with the law.

Note: Some publications or booklets provide a glossary at the end. This does not work well for readers with limited literacy skills because they may have difficulty switching back and forth from one section to another. They also may not understand the relationship between the text and the words defined in a separate section (National Cancer Institute, 2003). It is much better to define and explain unfamiliar terms in the text itself.

8. Use titles and headings.

Titles and headings prepare readers for what they will see next in the text. Telling readers what to expect helps them interpret the text that follows. Writing the heading in the form of a question is one way to engage readers. Questions encourage readers who are interested in the answers to continue reading. Using boldface for headings helps them stand out, as shown in example 1.6.

| Example 1.6 | Using Boldface Headings |

What is domestic violence?
Domestic violence is when one partner in a relationship controls the other through force, threats, or fear. Domestic violence occurs between married couples, unmarried couples who are living together, couples who are dating, and couples who are divorced or separated.

Who are the abusers?

Both men and women can be abusers, but most abusers are men. Abusers come from all cultures, races, religions, and classes.

9. Use one idea per paragraph.

Paragraphs are one way to organize written material. A paragraph should focus on one idea or topic. As we illustrate in the first part of example 1.7, a paragraph that combines several ideas is difficult to comprehend. Such paragraphs are especially baffling to people who are not fluent readers. The second part of example 1.7 illustrates how much less intimidating print looks, and how much easier it is to understand, when the text is broken up into short paragraphs separated by white space.

Example 1.7 **Paragraphs**

Women whose partners are abusing them may feel helpless. They may stay with their partners because they still love them. They may also feel ashamed. There are many forms of abuse. Physical abuse includes hitting, choking, kicking, and pushing. Mental abuse includes threats to harm the woman or her children. It also includes trying to control everything the woman does. Seeing abuse in the family is very harmful to children. This is true for both boys and girls. They may grow up to think that violence is a good way to deal with problems.

Women whose partners are abusing them may feel helpless. They may stay with their partners because they still love them. They may also feel ashamed.

There are many forms of abuse. Physical abuse includes hitting, choking, kicking, and pushing. Mental abuse includes threats to harm the woman or her children. It also includes trying to control everything the woman does.

Seeing abuse in the family is very harmful to children. This is true for both boys and girls. They may grow up to think that violence is a good way to deal with problems.

10. Use plenty of white space throughout the text.

Opening a booklet or brochure that is dense with text can be intimidating to anyone. When poor readers see long, unbroken blocks of writing, they may not even attempt to read the piece. You can encourage them to read your material if you separate short blocks of print with plenty of white space. For a booklet or brochure, be sure your page margins are at least half an inch wide and leave at least one inch of white space between columns of print.

11. Use short words and short sentences.

If you remember how difficult it was to decode words you did not recognize in the backward paragraph, you can understand the value of using short words and short sentences. Short words alone, however, do not guarantee readability, as we demonstrate in example 1.8. It is quite possible to use short words and still confuse your readers.

Example 1.8	Short Words Do Not Ensure Clarity

What is written on the printed page should make clear what is vital for readers to know. It should be written in a way that can be easily grasped by those who read it. The point should be gotten to quickly. If you do not do this, no one will want to read what you write and your meaning will not be clear even if all the words are short.

It is also true that you can write short sentences that few people will understand. Succinctness is not commensurate with perspicuity. To put that more clearly: brevity does not guarantee clarity.

12. Write in a conversational style.

We have known and worked with many college graduates who believe that written language should be different and distinct from spoken language. Readers with limited literacy skills are better able to understand a conversational style of writing. This means writing in a style that is similar to the way you talk, although without slang or colloquialisms. Conversational writing should sound natural if you read it out loud. In fact, when you are writing anything intended for clients, we suggest that you do read it aloud to find out if it sounds conversational.

13. Do not use contractions.

This is one exception to writing in a conversational style. Poor readers often skip the second half of a contracted word. If they skip the second half of a negative contraction, they will interpret a sentence to mean the opposite of what it says. For example, they might understand "Drugs *aren't* allowed in the shelter" to mean "Drugs *are* allowed in the shelter."

14. Be cautious about using graphics.

Graphics such as tables, charts, diagrams, and graphs are difficult for many people to interpret. They are especially confusing for readers with limited literacy skills (Doak et al., 1996; Flesch, 1974). For any material aimed at clients, you have a better chance of getting your message across in words than in graphic displays. If you feel you must use graphics, be sure to provide simple explanations of what they show.

15. Do not use colons and semicolons.

We have been advocating simple writing, and "simple writing makes complex punctuation unnecessary" (Glicken, 2008, p. 33). Readers with limited literacy skills are not familiar with semicolons and colons. There is no need to use semicolons when you are writing easy-to-read materials. Their primary function is to link two complete sentences together into one long sentence. It is much better to use shorter sentences with periods at the end.

Be cautious about using colons as well. Colons can be used to link two related sentences where the second sentence explains something about the first. This use of a colon may not be familiar to readers with limited literacy skills. It also increases the length of a sentence, as does using a colon to introduce a list within a sentence (see example 1.9). If you use bullets for the list of items after the colon, it is easier to read.

Example 1.9	Using Colons with Lists

To apply for services you must show us: your child's birth certificate, proof of address, a rent receipt, and gas and electric bills for the last three months.

To apply for services you must show us:

- your child's birth certificate
- proof of address
- a rent receipt
- gas and electric bills for the last three months

16. Do not use roman numerals

Many educated, fluent readers have trouble interpreting roman numerals. They should never be used in materials for clients.

We know from our own experience that the more you practice, the more natural it becomes to incorporate the guidelines for readability into your writing. And the more you incorporate the guidelines for readability into your own writing, the more you will notice the readability—or lack of readability—of all the print materials you encounter.

CONVINCING THE SKEPTICS

Presumably you're reading this book because you have an interest in making your agency's materials more readable. Be prepared for the possibility that others in your agency won't agree that this is necessary. We have worked with administrators and staff members who initially rejected suggestions to revise agency materials to improve their readability. Such individuals may be unaware of the mismatch between their agency's print materials and their clients' literacy skills. They may not realize that everyone associated with the agency would benefit from receiving material that is easily read and understood. Even if they recognize the benefits of improving readability, they may be concerned about the time and expense involved in making the necessary changes. And finally, they may mistakenly believe that simplifying information means dumbing it down.

If those responsible for approving the publication of your agency's print materials believe that easy-to-read materials reflect poorly on the expertise of an agency or organization, your first task will be to educate them. It will require tact, facts, and examples to convince these individuals that increasing the readability of the agency's print materials and electronic information will benefit clients as well as other stakeholders. The National Cancer Institute (2003) suggests the following for dealing with skeptics:

- Inform them before you begin writing or revising materials. Do not wait until you have a finished product to show them.
- Make sure that all simplified language and explanations you use are accurate.
- Work with the skeptics to develop solutions that satisfy their concerns without sacrificing readability.

If your agency's print materials were designed without readability in mind, as is true for many human service agencies, we hope you will develop an irresistible urge to alter them to improve their readability. Making these changes will require thought, planning, and practice, and possibly convincing the skeptics of the benefits of doing so. The next five chapters will help you plan, write, and evaluate easy-to-read print and online materials for your clients and other audiences with whom your agency uses the written word to communicate.

Finally, if you gave up on the backward paragraph presented in figure 1.1 earlier in the chapter, we have translated it (see figure 1.2). We hope that trying to read this message backward, and seeing it unscrambled, helps you understand what you can accomplish by providing your clients and others with readable materials.

Figure 1.2	**Backward Paragraph Unscrambled**

If you understand how difficult it is for people with limited literacy skills to read, you will know why it is so important to make sure your agency's print materials are easy to read. You may be having trouble reading this. Keep in mind how difficult it was to read this the next time you are responsible for writing something that your agency will give to clients. Is it possible that your agency can simplify its print materials to make them more readable? If so, this book will help you through that process.

REFERENCES

Allington, R. L., & McGill-Franzen, A. (2009). Comprehension difficulties among struggling readers. In S. E. Israel & G. G. Duffy (Eds.), *Handbook of research on reading comprehension* (pp. 551–568). New York, NY: Routledge.

American Counseling Association. (2005). *ACA Code of Ethics*. Retrieved from http://www .counseling.org/Resources/aca-code-of-ethics.pdf.

Arnold, C. L., Davis, T. C., Frempong, J. O., Humiston, S. G., Bocchini, A., Kennen, E. M., & Lloyd-Puryear, M. (2006). Assessment of newborn screening parent education materials. *Pediatrics, 117*(5), S320–S325.

Corley, M. A. (2003). Poverty, racism, and literacy. *ERIC Digest*. Retrieved from http://eric.ed.gov/PDFS/ ED475392.pdf.

Daneman, M. (1996). Individual differences in reading skills. In K. Barr, M. L. Kamil, P. B. Mosenthal, & P. D. Pearson (Eds.), *Handbook of reading research* (Vol. 2, pp. 512–538). Mahwah, NJ: Lawrence Erlbaum Associates.

Doak, C. C., Doak, L. G., & Root, J. (1996). *Teaching patients with low literacy skills* (2nd ed.). Philadelphia, PA: Lippincott. Available online: http://www.hsph.harvard.edu/health literacy/resources/doak-book/index .html.

Flesch, R. F. (1974). *The art of readable writing* (25th anniversary ed.). New York, NY: Collier Books.

Glicken, M. D. (2008). *A guide to writing for human service professionals*. Lanham, MD: Rowman & Little-field.

King, M., Winton, A., & Adkins, A. (2003). Assessing the readability of mental health Internet brochures for children and adolescents. *Journal of Child and Family Studies, 12*(1), 91–99. doi: 10.1023/A:1021362210470.

Kutner, M., Greenberg, E., & Baer, J. (2005). *National Assessment of Adult Literacy (NAAL): A first look at the literacy of American adults in the 21st century* (NCES 2006-470). Retrieved from National Center for Education Statistics, US Department of Education, http://nces.ed.gov/ NAAL/PDF/2006471_1.PDF.

Kutner, M., Greenberg, E., Jin, Y., & Paulsen, C. (2006). The health literacy of America's adults: Results from the 2003 National Assessment of Adult Literacy (NCES 2006-483). Retrieved from National Center for Education Statistics, US Department of Education, http://nces.ed.gov/ pubs2006/2006483.pdf.

Mavrogenes, N., Hanson, E., & Winkley, C. (1977). But can the client understand it? *Social Work, 22*, 110–112.

Mellard, D. F., & Fall, E. (2012). Component model of reading comprehension for adult education participants. *Learning Disability Quarterly, 35*(1), 10–23. doi: 10.1177/0731948711429197.

Mellard, D. F., Woods, K., & Fall, E. (2011). Assessment and instruction of oral reading fluency among adults with low literacy. *Adult Basic Education and Literacy Journal, 5*(1), 3–14.

National Association of Social Workers. (2008). *Code of Ethics of the National Association of Social Workers*. Washington, DC: Author. Retrieved from http://www.naswdc .org/pubs/code/code.asp.

National Cancer Institute. (2003). *Clear and simple: Effective print materials for low-literate readers*. Retrieved from http://www.cancer.gov/cancer topics/cancerlibrary/clear-and-simple/.

National Organization for Human Services. (2009). *Ethical standards for human service professionals*. Retrieved from http://www.national humanservices.org/ethical-standards-for-hs-professionals.

National Work Group on Literacy and Health. (1998). Communicating with patients who have limited literacy skills. Report of the National Work Group on Literacy and Health. *Journal of Family Practice, 46*, 168–176.

Rapp, D. N., van den Broek, P., McMaster, K. L., Kendeou, P., & Espin, C. A. (2007). Higher-order comprehension processes in strug-gling readers: A perspective for research and intervention. *Scientific Studies of Reading, 11*(4), 289–312.

Sabatini, J. P., Sawaki, Y., Shore, J. R., & Scarborough, H. S. (2010). Relationships among reading skills of adults with low literacy. *Journal of Learning Disabilities, 43*, 122138. doi: 10.1177/00222219409359343.

Shriver, K. A. (1997). *Dynamics in document design*. New York, NY: John Wiley.

Stanovich, K. E. (1996). Word recognition: Changing perspectives. In K. Barr, M. L. Kamil, P. B. Mosenthal, & P. D. Pearson (Eds.), *Handbook of reading research* (Vol. 2, pp. 418–452). Mahwah, NJ: Lawrence Erlbaum Associates.

US Census Bureau. (2006–2008). American Community Survey 3 Year Estimates. Retrieved from http://fact finder.census.gov/servlet/STTable?_ bm=y&-geo_id=01000US&-qr_ name=ACS_2008_3YR_G00_S1703 &-ds_name=ACS_2008_3YR_G00_ &-redoLog=false.

White, S., and Dillow, S. (2005). *Key concepts and features of the 2003 National Assessment of Adult Literacy* (NCES 2006-471). Retrieved from National Center for Education Statistics, US Department of Education, http://nces.ed.gov/NAAL/PDF/ 2006470_1.PDF.

Wilson, J. M., Wallace, L. S., & DeVoe, J. E. (2009). Are state Medicaid application enrollment forms readable? *Journal of Health Care for the Poor and Underserved, 20,* 423–431. doi: 10.1353/hpu.0.0127.

Yick, A. (2008). Evaluating readability of domestic violence information found on domestic violence state coalitions' websites. *Journal of Technology in Human Services, 26*(1), 67–74. doi: 10.1300/J017v26n01_05.

How to Make Your Writing Clear

Clear writing is hard for anyone to achieve. It results only from clear thinking and hard work.

—R. Gunning, *The Technique of Clear Writing*

We begin our discussion of clear writing with the following observation: professional education customarily encompasses instructional strategies and techniques that utilize unnecessarily esoteric inclusion of convoluted and exclusionary expressions of language devoid of clarity for those unassociated with one's professional linguistic articulations. You may have found this first sentence bewildering or even unintelligible. It's the kind of writing that leaves many readers confused and that we have seen far too often. What does the sentence mean? Perhaps this will be clearer: professional education programs teach you the language of your profession. Those who do not speak your language will not understand it.

There is a place for professional language. It allows you to communicate easily with colleagues from your own discipline or profession. It also makes you an insider. Unfortunately, you and your colleagues may lose sight of the fact that clients, the general public, and even professionals from other disciplines may not understand what you are saying. When you are writing for clients, it is especially important to use plain language rather than professional or agency terminology, jargon, or acronyms.

DEFINING PLAIN LANGUAGE

What is plain language? It is "clear, straightforward expression, using only as many words as are necessary. It is language that avoids obscurity, inflated vocabulary, and convoluted sentence construction. It is not baby talk, nor is it a simplified version of the English language. Writers of plain English let their audience concentrate on the message instead of being distracted by complicated language" (Eagleson, 1990, p. 4). You can use plain language to convey complex ideas. If you are not convinced of this now, we hope you will be by the time you finish this chapter.

The opposite of plain language is what we call fancy language. Fancy language includes long words, obscure words, and long, elaborate sentences that wind here, there, and everywhere. Fancy language may demonstrate that you are an intelligent, well-educated person with a large vocabulary, but it does not serve the needs of your clients. It can confuse or frustrate other readers as well. If you are accustomed to using long words and fluffing up what you write with extra words, it can be difficult to bring yourself to substitute plain language. Like any new habit, it takes practice.

IDENTIFYING JARGON

Jargon is the special language used within an organization, business, discipline, or profession that everyone within the group understands. Outsiders, however, will usually be mystified by this language. It can be as difficult for outsiders to translate jargon into plain English as it is to translate a foreign language. The more fluently you speak your professional and agency jargon, the more easily you can forget that others do not understand it. Jargon does not belong in anything you write for clients or the general public.

Here we list some of the jargon we have found in human service agency brochures and other materials intended for clients. You may recognize, and it's possible that you use, terms on this list. However, most clients and laypeople in the community will not know what they mean.

advocacy

agent for change

at-risk

autonomy

child-centered

developmental delays

developmentally appropriate activities

family dynamics

fatherhood initiatives

holistic

interpersonal skills

intimate partner

mentor

motor development

one-on-one support

positive emotional development

screening and assessment

social support

special needs

termination of assistance

AVOIDING ACRONYMS

Plain language means avoiding acronyms. Acronyms are abbreviations made up of the first letters of several words. Most acronyms that human service professionals use are not familiar to the average person. You may know that TANF is an acronym for Temporary Assistance for Needy Families or that SNAP stands for Supplemental Nutrition Assistance Program (and that SNAP was formerly known as food stamps). The average person would have no idea what these acronyms mean.

Like jargon, acronyms often become so common in your professional communications that you lose sight of the fact that they mean nothing to your clients and the general public. Additionally, the same acronym can have different meanings in different settings. For example, if you are a mental health professional, you may refer to borderline personality disorder as BPD. You might also use BPD as an acronym for bipolar disorder. To add to the potential confusion, if you happen to be a social work educator, you might know

BPD as the abbreviation for a professional organization called the Association of Baccalaureate Social Work Program Directors. Another acronym with several possible meanings is ASAP. Depending on your professional background, you might use it to stand for alcohol and substance abuse providers or the American Society for Adolescent Psychology, while the general public would presumably interpret it to mean "as soon as possible." You can see from these brief examples how easily communication can become confusing if you are not careful about your use of acronyms.

Although it takes longer to spell words out than to abbreviate them, it is best to spell them out. If you do include acronyms, especially in materials designed for clients or the general public, be sure to explain what they stand for the first time you use them. If you are going to use a phrase or title repeatedly, spell it out the first time and put the acronym in parentheses immediately following. Just be aware that unfamiliar acronyms, particularly those specific to your organization, will be hard for people to remember without looking back to see what they stand for.

Be aware, too, that often people do not read brochures straight through from beginning to end. They will scan from one section to another looking for what might be relevant to them. When people read material this way, they may miss the initial explanation of the acronym. To compensate for this you can make the first use, where you spell out the acronym, prominent so readers are more likely to see it. We think a better option is to use a simplified name for the entity you want to abbreviate (see the Federal Plain Language Guidelines at www.plainlanguage.gov).

As we illustrate in example 2.1, even when you spell out acronyms, they can be confusing and downright annoying to read. The text without acronyms is slightly longer, but people unfamiliar with the subject matter will be able to read and understand it more quickly.

Example 2.1	Text with and without Acronyms

Text with acronyms	**Text without acronyms**
The Happy Helpers Agency (HHA) Adult and Child Counseling Program (ACCP) serves adults, adolescents,	The Happy Helpers Agency Adult and Child Counseling Program serves adults, adolescents, and chil-

and children. ACCP provides long-term and crisis counseling. HHA also offers Special Child and Adolescent Therapy Groups (SCATG). For more information on ACCP and SCATG, call 000-555-1212.

dren. The Adult and Child Counseling Program provides long-term and crisis counseling. We also offer Special Child and Adolescent Therapy Groups. For more information on our programs, call 000-555-1212.

Although we just advised you not to use acronyms, there is the occasional exception where the acronym is more familiar than the term it stands for and thus a better choice than spelling out the words. For example, most people, especially those with limited literacy skills, would recognize the acronyms HIV and AIDS. They would probably not recognize *human immunodeficiency virus* as HIV or *acquired immune deficiency syndrome* as AIDS. Spelling out the words for these commonly recognized acronyms would decrease readability.

REPLACING FANCY LANGUAGE WITH PLAIN LANGUAGE

As you begin thinking about how you can improve the readability of your agency's print materials, you may want to begin a list of the acronyms, jargon, and fancy language from your brochures, flyers, booklets, application forms, and other materials. The next step is to find plain language substitutions. Example 2.2 provides three brief excerpts from materials designed for clients. We have underlined the jargon and fancy language and rewritten each example to illustrate how plain language makes comprehension easier.

Example 2.2   **Replacing Fancy Language with Plain Language**

Fancy Language Original

Our program provides a <u>framework</u> for planning <u>developmentally appropriate activities</u> for children as well as <u>creating an environment that fosters exploration and independent learning</u> through play.

Plain Language Revision

Our program plans activities that match children's ages and abilities. The play activities we offer can help children learn.

A *multifaceted approach* is used by our agency to <u>uniquely provide a wide range of interrelated programs</u> that address the many <u>challenges</u> faced by today's young people and their families.

Our agency offers many programs to help young people and their families with the problems they face.

Each guest is <u>granted an initial stay</u> of two months at the shelter. <u>Extensions</u> can be granted on a <u>case-by-case basis</u> through the <u>advocacy</u> of case management. Guests may be asked to leave before <u>the initial two-month stay</u> if that guest has <u>violated major facility rules.</u>

We allow all guests to stay at the shelter for two months. We allow some guests to stay longer if their case manager thinks it will help them. We may ask guests to leave immediately if they break major rules.

Exercise 2.1 is designed to help you begin developing your plain language vocabulary. It lists words and phrases commonly used in human service agency forms, applications, and publications meant for clients and asks you to come up with plain language substitutes. The plain language word substitution list in figure 2.1 at the end of the chapter includes the words in the exercise. Use it as a reference as you expand your plain language vocabulary.

| Exercise 2.1 | Plain Language for Human Services Professionals |

For each word or phrase, write down one or more plain language alternatives.

assistance _____

authorized representative _____

biannual _____

caregivers _____

confidentiality of communications _____

designate _____

documentation _____

eligibility determination _____

exempt _____

evaluate _____

interaction _____

intervention _____

legislation _____

mandated _____

necessitate _____

numerous _____

on a monthly basis _____

participate _____

prioritize _____

regulation _____

support services _____

transition _____

utilize _____

USING ACTIVE VOICE

You probably noticed in example 2.2 that the revised plain language versions were shorter than the original statements. This is partly because we used plain language. It is also the result of changing passive voice to active voice. If you are accustomed to writing in passive voice, you may not have noticed this. You may also find it difficult to distinguish active from passive voice. We will try to clarify and illustrate the difference.

Active voice is more specific, and usually more concise, than passive voice. This makes it the best choice for people with limited literacy skills, people for whom English is a second language, and individuals who have little prior knowledge of a topic (Spyridakis & Wenger, 1992). In active voice the subject of the sentence performs the action or causes the result that the sentence describes. Active voice helps readers interpret what they are reading *because* it specifically indicates who did what. Passive voice may not explain who did what. In passive voice the subject of the sentence does not perform the action or cause the result but instead is acted upon. Example 2.3 illustrates these differences.

Example 2.3	Comparing Active and Passive Voice
Active Voice	**Passive Voice**
Applicants must fill out the forms completely.	Forms are to be filled out completely. [Does not explain who is to fill out the forms.]
The neighbor called the police.	The police were called. [Does not explain who called the police.]
Mr. Penny hit Mrs. Penny.	Mrs. Penny was hit by Mr. Penny. [The subject, Mrs. Penny, did not perform the action.]

Two clues that can help you recognize passive voice are:

1. The use of a form of the verb *to be* with another verb, for example:
   - Free clothing *is* offered once a month.
   - Ten items of clothing *will be* provided to each family.
   - Many items of clothing *have been* donated.
2. The use of the word *by*, for example:
   - The clothing is offered *by* a local church.
   - Each family will be given ten items of clothing *by* the church.
   - Good quality clothing has been donated *by* the community.

As example 2.4 illustrates, passive voice usually requires more words than active voice to convey the same information because active voice is more direct. The fewer words you use to get your message across, the more quickly and easily your audience can read it.

Example 2.4	Active Voice Uses Fewer Words

Passive	Active
Your application for assistance has been received by our agency. For the application to be processed, additional forms must be submitted. Your application is being returned to you with the additional forms that are to be filled out. If you wish to have the application process completed, the application is to be returned. The required forms must be submitted with the application. [62 words]	Our agency has received your application for assistance. We cannot process the application until you submit additional forms. We are returning your application with the additional forms for you to fill out. To complete the application process, return this application and the required forms. [44 words]
Parent education materials are offered to all clients who are served by the program. [14 words]	The program offers parent education materials to all its clients. [10 words]
Clients are informed about our rules in an intake session. They are assigned a worker and an appointment is made. Their progress is monitored by their worker as they move through the program. [33 words]	We inform clients about our rules in an intake session. We assign them a worker and make an appointment. Their worker monitors their progress as they move through the program. [30 words]

Your high school, college, or graduate school instructors may have encouraged you to use passive voice out of a belief that it sounds more formal and professional. It is certainly more impersonal than active voice. When you write in passive voice, you can avoid using personal pronouns altogether. However, avoiding personal pronouns is not necessarily a good thing, especially when clients are your target audience. Your goal should be to connect with your audience rather than to distance yourself with impersonal language. Unless your goal is to avoid taking responsibility—as in the often used phrase "mistakes were made"—we advise you to use active voice consistently in your agency materials.

If you cannot bring yourself to use personal pronouns for agency materials, you can still write in active voice. You can use nouns such as "the agency," "the services," "the staff," and so on, although we encourage you to incorporate personal pronouns in your agency materials. As you can see in example 2.5, using active voice with personal pronouns such as *we, us,* or *our* gives the writing a more conversational tone. We will explain in chapter 3 why this is especially important for materials aimed at clients with limited literacy skills.

Example 2.5	**Using Active Voice with and without Personal Pronouns**
Active Voice without Personal Pronouns	**Active Voice with Personal Pronouns**
The program encourages parents to become involved in their children's education. Services include free tutoring for youth in grades 6–9. The program also provides life skills training. Parents can contact the staff for more information.	Our program encourages parents to become involved in their children's education. We offer free tutoring to youth in grades 6–9. We also provide life skills training. You can contact us for more information.

Figure 2.1	**Plain Language Word Substitution List**

Adapted from C. Baker, *Just say it! How to write for readers who don't read well* (Washington, DC: Push Literacy Action Now [PLAN], n.d.).

accessible	within reach
accompany	go with
accomplish	do
accordingly	so
accurate	correct or right
achieve	do; make
acquaint	get to know or meet with
actual	real
additional	more

adjacent to	next to
advantageous	helpful
adversely affect	hurt
affix	put
afford an opportunity	allow or let
ameliorate	improve
anticipate	expect
apparent	clear or plain
appreciable	many
approximately	about
ascertain	find out or learn
assist	help
assistance	help
at the present time	now
attached herewith is	here is
attempt	try
authorized representative	someone who can speak or sign for you
be in the position to	can
benefit	help
biannual	twice a year
capability	what you (or he, she, it, or they) can do
caregiver	person who cares for or takes care of
close proximity to	near
commence	start or begin
compensate	pay
comply with	follow
component	part
comprise	include or form or make up
concept	idea
concerning	about
confidentiality	privacy or keep what you tell us private

consequently	so
consider	think about
constitutes	is or makes up
construct	build or make
consult	ask or check with or talk to or meet
contains	has
contribute	give
conversation	talk
cooperate	help
correct	right
current residence	where you live or home address or address
currently	now
deem	think
deficiency	lack
delete	cut or drop or remove
demonstrate	show
depart	go or leave
designate	choose or name or tell
desire	wish
determine	decide or find
develop	grow or make or take place
detrimental	harmful
discontinue	end or drop or stop
discuss	talk about
disseminate	send out or give out or pass out or hand out
documentation	records or papers or forms
domicile	home or where you live
due to the fact that	because or since
during that time	while
economical	low-cost or cheap or does not cost a lot
effect	make

e.g.	for example
elect	choose or pick
eligible to enroll	can join or can sign up
eligibility determination	find out if we can help you
eliminate	cut or stop or drop
employ	use or hire
encounter	meet
encourage	urge
endeavor	try
ensure	make sure
enumerate	count
equitable	fair
equivalent	equal
establish	set up or prove or show
exempt	does not apply; is not true for you
evaluate	check or test or decide
evident	clear
examine	check or look at
excessive number of	too many
exhibit	show
expeditiously	quickly or fast or soon, right away
expend	pay out or spend
expense	cost or fee or price or how much you spend
explain	show or tell
facilitate	ease or help with
factor	reason or cause
failed to	did not
feasible	can do or workable
finalize	finish or complete
forfeit	give up or lose
for the purpose of	for

for the reason that	because
forward	send
function	act or work or role
fundamental	basic
furnish	give or send
has the capability	can
henceforth	from now on
herein	here
however	but
identical	same
identify	name or find or show
i.e.	that is
if you require assistance	if you need help
immediately	now or right away
impacted	changed
implement	do or follow or put in place or carry out
in accordance with	by or under
in an effort to	to
inasmuch as	since
inception	start
in conjunction with	with
incorporate	combine, join
incorrect	wrong
incumbent upon	must
indicate	show, write down
initial	first
initiate	start
in lieu of	instead of
in order that	so
in order to	to
inquiries	questions

in regard to	about, on
interaction	working together or meeting with
intervention	help or a program to help
in the amount of	for
in the course of	in or during
in the event that	if
in the majority of cases	usually
in the near future	soon
in view of	since
in view of the fact	because
it is essential	must
it is requested that	please
justify	prove
large numbers of	many
legislation	law
limited number	few
limitations	limits
locate	find
locality	place
lucid	clear
magnitude	size
maintain	keep
majority	most
mandated	required or you must do this
modify	change
monitor	check or watch or keep track of
necessitate	force or cause
notify	tell or let know
numerous	many or a lot
objective	goal or aim
observe	see

obtain	get
on a monthly basis	monthly or every month
on the basis of	because or based on
operate	run or work
operational	working
optimum	best
option	choice or way
participate	do or take part in
perform	do
permit	let
personnel	people or staff
pertaining to	about or of or on
portion	part
possess	have or own
preclude	prevent
premises	building
prepared	ready
previous	before, past
prior to	before
prioritize	rank or decide what is important
probability	chance
procedures	rules or ways
proceed	do or go on
proficiency	skill
promptly	right away
provide	give or say
provided that	if
purchase	buy
reason for	why
receive	get
reduce	cut

regarding	about or of or on
registration	sign-up
regulation	rule
relating to	about or on
relocate	move
remain	stay
remainder	rest
remuneration	pay
render	give or make
request	ask
require	must or need
rescind	take back
retain	keep
return	go back
review	check or go over
selection	choice
similar	like
solicit	ask for
state	say
strategize	plan
statutory	by law or legal
submit	send or give
subsequent	next
subsequent to	after
subsequently	later
substantial	large or strong
sufficient	enough
support services	services that help; what we can do to help you
terminate	end or stop
therefore	so
this office	we

transition	change or move to
transmit	send or give
transpire	happen
until such time as	until
utilize	use
validate	confirm
value	cost or worth
vehicle	car or truck
verbatim	word for word
via	in or on or through
viable	working or workable
warrant	call for
we are in a position to	we can
whenever	when
whereas	since
with reference to	about
with regard to	about
witness	see
you are obligated to	you must

REFERENCES

Baker, C. (n.d.). *Just say it! How to write for readers who don't read well.* Washington, DC: Push Literacy Action Now (PLAN).

Eagleson, R. D. (1990). *Writing in plain English.* Canberra, Australia: Australian Government Publication Service.

Gunning, R. (1968). *The technique of clear writing.* New York, NY: McGraw-Hill.

Spyridakis, J. H., & Wenger, M. J. (1992). Writing for human performance: Relating reading research to document design. *Technical Communication, 39*(2), 202–215.

Planning Ahead for Readability

A good plan is like a road map: it shows the final destination and usually the best way to get there.
—**H. Stanley Judd, quoted in Cichocki and Irwin,** *Organization Design*

The time you invest in planning can mean the difference between reaching the audience you want to reach with information they can use and simply handing out information that few can read, let alone understand. Taking the time to review existing materials and thoughtfully and deliberately plan new ones will increase the probability that your audiences will be willing and able to read the materials you give them.

Before you begin writing or revising anything, it is helpful to take the time to assess who you want to reach—your target audience—and why you want to reach them—your purpose. It may be tempting to develop a brochure or flyer for "everyone," but if you take a one-size-fits-all approach, your message may not convey information specific enough for any of the audiences you're trying to reach. Additionally, a generic piece "assumes that individuals can and will sift through the parts of these materials that do not apply to them to find and consume that material which does" (Kreuter, Strecher, & Glassman, 1999). This approach is counterproductive for individuals with limited literacy skills. They will be unable to find the information that would be useful to them. It's worth remembering that there is often a wealth of detailed information available to those who want to explore your agency's programs or the issues you deal with in depth. What is too often lacking is clearly and concisely written information that people with limited literacy skills can easily understand.

Investing a bit of time and effort to lay the groundwork before you write new materials or revise existing ones will pay off in increased readability. This initial planning need not be time-consuming or cumbersome, and it will clarify your thinking so that you can formulate clear messages for specific audiences. It will help you avoid the common pitfalls of creating materials that do not appeal to your target audience(s), deliver confusing messages, or fail to state clearly what your target audience needs to know.

DEFINING YOUR PURPOSE

Whether you are planning to revise existing materials or create new ones, the first step is to define the purpose of the material. Once you define your purpose, you can identify your target audience or audiences, assess what they need to know, and eliminate any unnecessary information that may detract from your message. A good way to begin is to ask yourself what goal or outcome you would like to see. Another way of looking at this is to begin with the end in mind. What change do you want to see in those who read your message? Are you looking for a change in behavior or increased knowledge about a specific topic? Do you want to persuade your readers to donate money or volunteer time? The more specifically you can define what you wish to accomplish, the better you will be able to identify specific audiences and craft messages designed to achieve the desired outcome. For example, if you are developing a brochure to describe your agency's services, your purpose might include some or all of the following:

- motivating eligible individuals to apply for services
- informing current clients about rules or behavioral expectations
- soliciting new volunteers
- obtaining donations of money or goods
- increasing the number of callers to your hotline
- increasing knowledge about specific issues, such as child abuse, adoption, mental illness, sexual assault, etc.
- reducing the incidence of problems, such as teen pregnancy, childhood obesity, or juvenile delinquency, in your community

Defining your purpose will prepare you for the next step in your planning process: identifying the target audience or audiences you must reach to achieve your purpose.

IDENTIFYING YOUR TARGET AUDIENCES

Your target audience(s) are all those individuals, organizations, and groups you wish to reach. Depending on your purpose, they could include clients, prospective clients, agency staff, current volunteers, prospective volunteers, community members, professionals in other agencies, current donors, prospective donors, current board members, and prospective board members.

As an example, let's say one purpose you have defined is to motivate individuals in need of your agency's services to apply for them. Prospective clients will need information about the services your agency offers, who is eligible for specific services, and how to contact the agency in order to request more information or apply for services. Information about what volunteers do and the kind of donations your agency needs or what a specific monetary donation can pay for will be of no interest to this audience.

If your purpose is to motivate prospective clients to apply for services, they may not be the only audience you want to target. You may also choose to target other professionals who refer clients. The general public could also be a target audience because community members might suggest that a family member or friend seek assistance from your agency.

Reaching Diverse Audiences

If your community is diverse, a target audience of clients or prospective clients is likely to be diverse. This means it is important to do enough homework to find out what subgroups make up that audience. Are there ethnic, cultural, racial, or linguistic differences you should take into account? Are there gender, age, or sexual orientation distinctions that differentiate subgroups within your target audience?

If you wish to reach diverse ethnic and cultural communities, it is important to develop culturally appropriate materials and messages. Culturally appropriate materials take into account "the language, thoughts, communications, actions, customs, beliefs, values, and institutions of racial, ethnic, religious, or social groups" (US Department of Health and Human Services Office of Minority Health, 2001, p. 5). To write culturally appropriate materials, you must be familiar with your target audience's cultural values, practices, and beliefs. You also need to know what barriers might prevent them from seeking your agency's services or participating in programs your agency offers. Among some groups, for example, there is stigma associated with asking "outsiders" for help. If you do not take all of these factors into account, you may miss the opportunity to reach culturally diverse groups with your messages.

How do you create culturally appropriate materials? If you are unfamiliar with the groups you wish to reach, you will need to do some research. The AMC Cancer Research Center (1994) suggests a variety of ways to gather information about the subgroups that make up your target audience. You might begin by reading a few articles. This can be a useful first step in familiarizing yourself with communities and populations that you don't know much about. It will give you an overview of cultural values and practices, family structure, religious beliefs, language, and other factors you may need to take into consideration when trying to reach particular groups.

Reading should be only the first step, however. It is not a substitute for seeking information directly from members of the groups you intend to target. Members of your target audience are the best source of information about that audience. Local groups, organizations, and professionals that work with your target audience should be able to provide you with advice. They may also be able to help you find individuals who would be willing to talk with you informally, answer specific questions, participate in surveys, or give you feedback on the cultural suitability of your materials (AMC Cancer Research Center, 1994; Centers for Disease Control and Prevention, 2009).

If you are launching a new program and developing materials to promote it, this kind of research is especially important. If you are revising existing materials that were developed without researching the target audience, it is equally important to gather enough information to be sure your materials focus on points the audience will be interested in and receptive to. Finally, learning about your target audience will keep you from presenting information in ways they might find irrelevant or offensive.

Our favorite example of what can happen if you don't educate yourself about cultural nuances is not explicitly related to developing print materials, but it is instructive. Frontier Airlines is a low-cost carrier that serves cities and towns across the United States. Frontier paints the tails of its planes with colorful images of its "spokesanimals," one of which is Ollie the Great Gray Owl. If you were a member of a Native American tribe for whom the owl is a symbol of death, would you board a plane with the image of an owl on the tail? Knowing your audience can make a real difference.

Using Culturally Acceptable Terms

When you are trying to reach diverse audiences, it is important to use the same terms that members of those audiences use to identify themselves. Be aware that even within identifiable groups, there are differences. Do not assume you know which terms to use unless you have spoken with people about their preferences. For example, some groups may refer to themselves as black while others prefer African American. Unless you ask, you won't know if people in your area call themselves Native Americans or American Indians, or whether they prefer to be known as members of a particular tribe.

The same is true for the terms *Latino/Latina* and *Hispanic*, which are often used interchangeably to describe a very diverse population. These individuals may share a connection with the Spanish language and a strong family orientation, but they have cultural, ethnic, linguistic, and religious differences. Some of these individuals strongly prefer to be known as either Hispanic or Latino/Latina. Some have no preference. Others refer to themselves by their country of origin, for example, Cuban, Puerto Rican, Mexican, Dominican, and so on (Passel & Taylor, 2009). The important thing is to determine if your audience has a preference and, if so, what it is.

Writing for Older Adults

We recognize that older adults differ greatly individually, culturally, and linguistically. Additionally, there is no absolute, agreed-upon age at which individuals become "older adults." While 60 or 65 is generally the age at which people are labeled "older adults," it is more important to gauge the functional age of your target audience than to define them solely by the number of birthdays they have celebrated. That said, there are some specific factors to consider when your target audience includes older adults.

Although individuals do age at different rates, many older adults experience changes in their vision that can make reading more difficult. Small print or lack of contrast between print and background can make reading especially problematic. Materials that use large print and plenty of white space and that are limited to need-to-know information will make reading easier for older audiences. You want to be sure there is plenty of contrast between the print and the background (for example, black ink, white or off-white background). Even your choice of paper can affect older adults' ability to read print. Glossy paper, which may look polished and professional in a brochure, reflects light, and this makes it harder for older eyes to decipher the print. It is much better to use paper that does not have a shiny finish.

Some cognitive skills decrease in older adults as well. They may process information more slowly than younger individuals, experience difficulty concentrating on details, or have trouble finding specific information in a long document (Stevens, 2003). Being concise, defining your terms, and using plenty of white space will help older adults compensate for declining cognitive skills, as will using active voice. For example, "Applications will be accepted between 8:00 a.m. and 5:00 p.m." is not as clear and direct as "Please submit your application between 8:00 a.m. and 5:00 p.m."

GETTING DOWN TO BUSINESS

You may find it helpful, before you begin writing or revising specific materials, to use the sample planning worksheet in figure 3.1 to articulate your purpose, identify potential target audiences and literacy concerns, and note any special diversity-related considerations such as language, culture, ethnicity, and age. Remember that if you are targeting clients, prospective clients, or the general public, literacy is likely to be an issue for significant segments of those populations. When you are developing materials for any of those audiences, we encourage you to follow the guidelines for creating readable materials in chapter 1.

Figure 3.1	Sample Planning Worksheet

Purpose of Material _____

Use the checklist below to identify your target audience(s) and whether literacy is an issue. Note specific language and diversity issues that you will want to attend to when writing for each audience.

Target Audience(s)	Limited Literacy	Language and Diversity Notes
☐ Current clients	☐	_____
☐ Prospective clients	☐	_____
☐ Volunteers	☐	_____
☐ Prospective volunteers	☐	_____
☐ Community/general public	☐	_____
☐ Human service professionals	☐	_____
☐ Other professionals	☐	_____
☐ Donors	☐	_____
☐ Board members	☐	_____
☐ Prospective board members	☐	_____
☐ Other _____	☐	_____

Once you have identified your purpose, your target audiences, and any diversity and language issues related to each target audience, it's time to focus on writing your message. You might not have thought about this prior to picking up this book, but we believe the most difficult audience to write for is individuals with limited literacy skills. One issue is style: the words you choose, the sentences you construct, and the tone you adopt. As we discussed in chapter 1, you must rethink much of what you take for granted as an educated reader and writer in order to improve the readability of your writing. The second, and equally critical issue, is content: what you write about. Because it is so difficult for people with limited literacy skills to gather information from print materials, they must be able to grasp immediately that your materials and your message are relevant to their needs and interests. The message must focus only on those needs and interests rather than requiring readers to pick out what they need to know from text containing other information that does not address their concerns.

If you have identified more than one target audience, the next question is whether you should create more than one piece. To help you determine this, consider what each audience needs to know for you to achieve your purpose. Are you trying to recruit more clients directly? Are you aiming for professionals in other agencies who might refer clients to you? Do you want to reach people who will donate money or goods or volunteer their time? Thinking this through will help you identify how many different audiences you have and which messages will be relevant to each audience. Specific information about programs, services, and eligibility criteria would be useful to clients and potential clients. It would also be helpful for other professionals who might make referrals and to friends and family members of potential clients. Your purpose in targeting volunteers and donors is quite different. You want them to assist your agency in specific ways. A concise summary of programs and services would probably be more relevant than details about how to apply for services. You can devote more of the text instead to describing what volunteers do or what a donation can support.

We recognize that it requires both additional time and additional money to create more than one piece. If you don't have the resources to do this, and clients are among those you are trying to reach, you will be wise to write the content as clearly and simply as possible. If the piece is readable enough for those with limited literacy skills to comprehend, you can be sure that most people who pick it up will be able to make sense of it. Furthermore, if they can quickly read it and grasp its meaning, they are unlikely to object that it took them only a short time to read.

Separating Need to Know from Nice to Know

Whether you have one audience or multiple audiences, you must be able to identify what the audience needs to know for the material to accomplish its purpose. This requires a certain amount of self-discipline because it is critical, and often quite difficult, to separate the information your audience needs to know from the information you think it would be nice for them to know. This is important no matter who your audience is, but it is especially so when you are writing for those with limited literacy skills. When we know a lot about a topic, we often assume that others will be delighted—or at least interested—in as many details as we are willing and able to provide. Not so.

Let us illustrate for you the difference between need to know and nice to know. You probably use a microwave oven at home or at work. If you're like most people, you probably can't explain how a microwave oven works. But do you need to know how it works in order to use it? Fortunately (at least for most of us), you do not. All you need to know is how to push the buttons. If you had to read through a long, technical explanation of how a microwave oven cooks to find out which buttons to push to heat your lunch, you might decide it wasn't worth using. Remember this example when you are sorting out what your audience needs to know. Do not allow yourself to tell them the equivalent of how the microwave works.

So how do you decide what your audience needs to know? If you've done your planning and identified your purpose and your target audience, you have a guide for assessing what the audience needs to know. If the information is critical to the outcome, include it. If not, let it go. Marketing professionals employ a strategy called the elevator speech or elevator pitch. The goal is to be able to get your message across verbally in the amount of time it would take to ride a few floors on an elevator. The elevator speech is what you are left with when you have distilled your message down to its essence. Writing the equivalent of the elevator speech means stripping away excess, nice-to-know information. If you're concerned that a short piece with basic information will not be informative enough for everyone, you can always include a line that says, "For more information about what we do, contact us at . . ." or you can refer people who want more details to your agency's website or a more detailed publication.

You may well have a great deal of detailed information in the materials your agency currently distributes. What you most likely do not have is simple information that clients, in particular, can understand. If they do not understand the written information you give them, you may not get a second chance to provide them with that information. Remember that even people with high-level literacy skills may not want to read reams of information about topics in which they have only moderate interest.

Now let us focus for a moment on all the nice-to-know information that is so often included in agency materials. We define nice-to-know information as any details that do not directly contribute to the message your audience needs to know to accomplish your purpose. Nice-to-know information adds more words. The longer the piece, the less likely those with limited literacy skills (and those with limited interest) are to try to read it. Remember, too, that readers with limited literacy skills have trouble pulling meaning from print. They may be unable to separate what they need to know from the details that surround it even if they are interested in the subject matter.

You can, no doubt, describe in detail what your agency does and the issues you deal with professionally. It can be tempting to share your knowledge and expertise in print and online. You may be eager to let everyone know about the credentials or degrees your staff members hold and how many years your agency has been in business. But does your target audience need to know this for the piece to accomplish its purpose? If not, leave it out. No matter who your target audience is, the less you write, the more likely it is they will read the whole thing.

If you want to inform prospective clients about how your agency can help them, these are the kinds of things they need to know:

- the services your agency offers
- whether they can apply themselves or must have a referral
- how to contact the agency
- if they need an appointment or can walk in for services
- the hours the agency and/or phone lines are open
- any documentation they need to apply for services
- basic eligibility criteria such as age, financial circumstances, or family circumstances
- whether services are free, covered by Medicaid or other insurance, or charged according to set fees or a sliding scale

The information that clients need to know would also be relevant for professionals in other agencies who might refer clients to your agency. It would help them decide whether a referral was appropriate. This information could also be useful to individuals in the community who need the services you provide or who know someone who could benefit from your services.

ASSESSING AND REWRITING EXISTING MATERIALS

Rather than creating new materials, you may choose to rewrite existing materials to make them more readable. Before you begin a rewrite, you should make sure you can define the purpose of the piece and identify the target audience. If the content is consistent with the purpose and appropriate for the target audience, you can concentrate on rewriting it to improve readability. If the purpose is unclear, or you find you are dealing with a one-size-fits-all brochure that targets "everyone," it will require more than rewriting. You can begin the process of making it more readable and useful to the people you are trying the reach by listing the information or topics it contains. Example 3.1 is a list of topics found in a brochure from an agency that offers domestic violence and sexual assault services.

Example 3.1

List of Topics in a Sexual Assault/Domestic Violence Brochure

- a list of agency services and hotline phone numbers
- definitions of domestic violence
- descriptions of types of abuse and abusive behaviors
- a definition of a safety plan
- an explanation a safety plan
- a quote from a survivor about what it was like to live with an abusive partner
- a definition of rape
- a definition of sexual assault
- descriptions of types of rapists
- descriptions of date rape drugs
- how to respond if someone you know is a victim of domestic violence or sexual assault
- the agency's address, phone numbers, and website
- a definition of stalking
- a statement that anyone can be a victim

- a form to be returned with a donation, a request for information about volunteering, or a request for a speaker
- a quote from a child who witnessed domestic violence
- information about various issue-awareness months and a website for more information
- a description of what agency volunteers do
- a request for donations and speaking invitations
- information about agency satellite office locations
- a request for donations of goods
- information about services for sexual assault victims

The brochure covers a multitude of topics in what appears to be an attempt to reach multiple audiences: victims and survivors of domestic violence and sexual assault, potential volunteers, victims of stalking, potential donors, and community members who may know a victim. We had no idea what to read first, which we suspect would be true for many people. The most vulnerable of the intended audiences—victims and survivors, and especially those with limited literacy skills—are the least likely to have the capacity or the will to find the information they need.

How can this be fixed? Let us look first at the multiple purposes the agency is trying to accomplish with this brochure. They include:

1. Improving the safety of victims and survivors of domestic violence by increasing their knowledge and motivating them to contact the agency for services and information
2. Increasing the well-being of victims and survivors of sexual assault by increasing knowledge about sexual assault and motivating them to contact the agency for services and information
3. Encouraging community members to reach out to victims of domestic violence
4. Recruiting volunteers
5. Soliciting donations of money and goods

This agency might be wise to provide two brochures, one for victims, survivors, and the general public and another for potential volunteers and donors. If they were to decide to do this, the next step would be to define the purpose of each brochure and identify what each audience needs to know. Let's begin with an audience of victims, survivors, and the general public. If the purpose is to improve victims' safety and well-being, they need to know:

- what behaviors the terms *domestic violence* and *sexual assault* describe
- how the agency can help someone who has experienced sexual assault or domestic violence
- how to contact the agency

If the purpose for a second brochure is to recruit volunteers and solicit donations, these audiences need to know:

- whom the agency helps
- the services and programs they provide
- what they can do to support the agency and its mission

If your agency distributes brochures or other materials with multiple purposes that are not targeted to specific audiences, you can go through the same process before you attempt to rewrite them. When you begin the process of rewriting, do not expect to rewrite the entire piece only once. You will probably need to make several revisions as you attempt to incorporate the guidelines for readability. All writing benefits from revision, but this is especially true if your goal is to create materials that are easy to read, because writing simply and clearly is not a simple or easy task.

To help you with the process of rewriting and revising, we have adapted a step-by-step process originally created for rewriting public health information (Rudd, Kaphingst, Colton, Gregoire, & Hyde, 2004, p. 199). It can be used for informational pamphlets, educational materials, facility rules and regulations, eligibility information, application forms, and informed consent documents. We suggest you regard a first draft to be a starting place for the finished product. Much of the time, particularly as you try to change your customary writing style, you will find yourself including professional language, long sentences, and nice-to-know information in early drafts. We encourage you to use the guide in figure 3.2 for rewriting existing materials and revising early drafts of new materials. It will help you identify what you can change to improve readability.

| Figure 3.2 | Guide for Rewriting and Revising |

1. Remove all nice-to-know content.
2. Highlight, circle, or underline all long, uncommon, and complex words in the text.*
3. Identify everyday words (i.e., plain language) to replace highlighted words. There are times when several short words can be easier to understand than one long or uncommon or complex word.
4. Replace highlighted words with everyday words.
5. Rewrite complex sentences. If necessary, divide them into two or three shorter sentences.
6. Rewrite all sentences in active voice.
7. Insert words such as "we," "our," and "you" to personalize the material. This will also help you change passive voice to active voice.

*Complex words include those with prefixes (e.g., re-, de-, pre-, intra-, contra-) and suffixes (e.g., -ify, -ate, -ness, -ization, -ity), as well as fancy words such as utilize or pertaining to.

In example 3.2, we have applied the guide in figure 3.2 to an excerpt from a flyer intended to recruit new clients for an early intervention program for young children. The target audience is low-income parents of infants and toddlers with, or at risk for, developmental delays. In the first column we have underlined the words that need simplification or replacement and bracketed the nice-to-know information.

What prospective clients need to know about the early intervention program is that it can help them and their children cope with some of the difficulties they face. The fact that the professionals who work for the program include early intervention specialists, developmental psychologists, occupational therapists, physical therapists, and speech therapists may be nice to know but is unlikely to be relevant or meaningful to parents who do not know what these professionals do.

Once we have removed the nice-to-know information, we can concentrate on replacing words, rewriting sentences, and changing the impersonal tone to one that speaks directly to parents. In the second column we identified plain language to replace the terms and professional jargon the average person, regardless of their literacy skills, might not understand.

In the third column you can compare the original material with a revision written in active voice using plain language, personal pronouns, and short sentences. We also divided the material into short paragraphs.

Example 3.2	Early Intervention Program Brochure Excerpt	
Original	**Replacements for professional terms and jargon**	**Revision**
Early intervention involves a variety of services offered by our program that provide a good or head start for children who may be at risk for developmental delays. Parents and professionals are encouraged to work	early intervention: offering help to parents with babies and young children developmental delays: a child not doing things such as sitting, walking, or talking at the age when most children do those things	Do you have a child with special needs? Has your child been slow to do things like sitting, walking or talking? If so, our program can help. Our staff works together with parents. We can help you help your child learn new skills through play.

together to <u>enhance the development</u> of infants and toddlers through play and [interactions with others]. The role of the family in their child's development and <u>service planning</u> is nurtured. [The professionals employed by our agency include early intervention specialists, developmental psychologists, occupational therapists, physical therapists, and speech therapists.] Caring for a child with <u>special needs</u> can mean additional stress for families. A very important part of <u>early intervention</u> is <u>family support</u> and education to assist families in meeting their needs and those of their child.

enhance the development: help your child learn new skills

service planning: setting up a plan for your family that says who will do what

family support: work with your family to help your children do better

We can help you decide what your family and your child need. We know that taking care of a child with special needs can be stressful. We will work with you to make a plan for meeting your needs and your child's needs.

TRANSLATING ENGLISH INTO OTHER LANGUAGES

It is common practice, in culturally diverse communities, for agencies to translate their materials into other languages. In an ideal world, agencies would have the resources to develop culturally appropriate materials in the languages spoken by their intended audiences. In the less-than-perfect world most of us inhabit, materials often get translated from the original English into a second language. If you must translate, do be sure you are translating text that is clear and easy to understand in English. If it's not clear in English, it won't be clear when translated into another language.

The person you choose to do the translation should speak the language and be familiar enough with your audience to understand cultural and linguistic nuances. Ideally, the translator should be a native speaker of the language, have at least ten years translation experience, and be certified by a recognized institution (Centers for Disease Control and Prevention, 2009). A translator who is familiar with your audience's language and culture will help ensure that you do not unintentionally offend your audience. For example, the relatively informal, conversational style of writing we recommend for English-speaking audiences may not be culturally appropriate. "For some languages and some audiences, it may be important to show respect by using a more formal and distant style" (McGee, 2010, Section 5, Part 11, p. 6).

Whatever you do, be sure you do not end up with a literal translation of the original English. A literal translation may amuse or bewilder your audience. It most certainly will not convey your message effectively. To be effective, the translation must use the expressions, phrases, and terms your audience uses; otherwise it may be unacceptable or offensive. You may also want to spend a bit of time helping the translator understand the basics of writing for people with limited literacy skills so that the translated content does not inadvertently become more complex.

If you do not speak the language(s) into which you are having your materials translated, you will not be able to verify whether the translated material achieves your intended purpose. If this is the case, the Centers for Disease Control and Prevention (CDC) recommends having someone other than the original translator translate the material from the second language back into English. This allows you to read it and make sure that the original meaning and tone did not get lost in translation. The CDC also recommends avoiding the following common pitfalls:

- Do not translate English slang or idioms literally.
- Do not translate into a dialect unless you know your audience uses it.

- Do not leave out foreign language characters or accent marks, because these omissions can change the meaning of words and sentences.

- Do be sure, if you list a phone number to call for more information, that you have staff members who are fluent in the language to take calls. If they are available only during certain hours, list those hours. (2009, p. 26)

REFERENCES

AMC Cancer Research Center. (1994). *Beyond the brochure: Alternative approaches to health communication*. Denver, CO: Author. Retrieved from http://www.cdc.gov/cancer/nbccedp/pdf/amcbeyon.pdf.

Centers for Disease Control and Prevention. (2009). *Simply put: A guide for creating easy-to-understand materials* (3rd ed.). Retrieved from http://www.cdc.gov/healthliteracy/pdf/simply_put.pdf.

Cichocki, P., & Irwin, C. (2011). *Organization design: A guide to building effective organizations*. London, UK: Kogan Page.

Kreuter, M., Strecher, V., & Glassman, B. (1999). One size does not fit all: The case for tailoring print materials. *Society of Behavioral Medicine, 21*, 276–83. doi: 10.1023/A:1021362210470.

McGee, J. (2010). *Toolkit for making written material clear and effective*. Retrieved from http://www.cms.gov/Outreach-and-Education/Outreach/WrittenMaterialsToolkit/index.html.

Passel, J., & Taylor, P. (2009). *Who's Hispanic?* Retrieved from http://www.pewhispanic.org/files/reports/111.pdf.

Rudd, R. E., Kaphingst, K. A., Colton, T., Gregoire, J., & Hyde, J. (2004). Rewriting public health information in plain language. *Journal of Health Communications, 9*, 195–206. doi: 10.1080/10810730490447039.

Stevens, B. (2003). How seniors learn. *Issue Brief, 4*(9). Retrieved from http://www.mathematica-mpr.com/PDFs/howseniors.pdf.

US Department of Health and Human Services Office of Minority Health. (2001). *National standards for culturally and linguistically appropriate services in health care*. Retrieved from http://www.gpo.gov/fdsys/search/pagedetails.action?granuleId=&packageId=GPO-STYLE MANUAL-2008&fromBrowse=true.

How to Achieve and Measure Readability

So likewise ye, except ye utter by the tongue words easy to be understood, how shall it be known what is spoken?

—1 Corinthians 14:9

Whether you are drafting new materials or revising existing ones, you will need tools to assess whether your words are "easy to be understood" (although we would, of course, quibble with the use of passive voice in that phrase). Without assessing the readability of your materials, you will not know if they have "that quality . . . which induces a reader to go on reading" (McLaughlin, 1974, p. 367). And there are many factors to consider if you wish to induce readers with limited literacy skills to go on reading long enough to get your message.

The first factor—and many people think it is the only factor—that determines readability is reading grade level. Certainly reading grade level is a key component of readability, but it is just a starting point. Readability involves far more than simply measuring reading grade level; however, we will start with that.

USING READABILITY FORMULAS TO MEASURE READING GRADE LEVELS

All methods of measuring readability use formulas that assess sentence length and word difficulty to mathematically calculate and assign numerical grade level scores. Because each formula uses a slightly different method to analyze text, the results will vary slightly from formula to formula. All, however, "provide a reasonably accurate grade level (typically plus or minus one grade level)" (Doak, Doak, & Root, 1996, p. 44). In other words, they are a sensible first step to take to determine the approximate reading level of your material.

Readability formulas predict reading difficulty for a particular piece of written material, but you cannot depend on formulas alone to tell you whether a document is readable for an audience with limited literacy skills. No readability formula is perfect nor does a low reading grade level guarantee that your target audience will be able to comprehend what you write. However, if you can achieve a reading level of eighth grade or lower, and you incorporate the guidelines for readability we presented in chapter 1, you will be well on your way to creating materials that most people can read and understand.

Online Readability Calculators

There are a number of free online readability calculators. If your text is saved on a computer, you can cut and paste excerpts of text and get an estimate of reading grade levels in a few seconds. For example, www.ReadabilityFormulas.com offers access to a dozen readability calculators along with brief explanations of what each measures. This rather busy-looking website also provides links to a number of articles on improving readability.

The website www.Online-Utility.org analyzes the readability of text and gives you results from a number of different readability formulas. In addition to providing grade levels based on multiple formulas, it suggests which sentences you might rewrite to improve readability.

Calculating Readability by Hand

If you are revising existing materials for which you have only hard copies, do not despair. There is a relatively quick and simple method for calculating the readability of text. If your agency uses materials created elsewhere or you do not have the text stored on a computer, these methods will give you a reasonable estimate of reading grade level.

The SMOG (Simple Measure of Gobbledygook) Readability Formula (figure 4.1) is a "sublimely simple procedure that really does predict readability" (McLaughlin, 1974, p. 367). SMOG is our preferred formula for calculating reading levels without a computer precisely because of its simplicity. While no formula is perfect, SMOG is widely used and has been called "the gold standard readability measure" (Fitzsimmons, Michael, Hulley, & Scott, 2010, p. 294). In example 4.1 we have applied SMOG to a thirty-sentence sample. The words with three or more syllables are underlined.

| Figure 4.1 | The SMOG Readability Formula |

Step 1: Select ten sentences in a row from the beginning of your material, then select ten in a row from the middle, and ten from near the end for a total of thirty sentences. Here is what counts as a sentence:

- A sentence is any string of words punctuated by a period, exclamation point, or question mark.
- If a sentence has a colon followed by a listing, count each part of the list *with* the beginning phrase as a sentence.

Step 2: Count every word with three or more syllables in each group of sentences; if the same words appear more than once, count them each time they appear. The easiest way to count syllables is to pronounce the words aloud. The rules for counting words are:

- Count hyphenated words as one word.
- Say numbers out loud and count the number of syllables pronounced (for example, "17" = three syllables).
- Count proper nouns.
- Count the number of syllables for abbreviated words as the whole word they represent (for example, "Dec." = December = three syllables).

Step 3: Add the total number of words with three or more syllables. Use the SMOG conversion table to find the grade level.

SMOG Conversion Table

Word Count	Grade Level
0–2	4
3–6	5
7–12	6
13–20	7
21–30	8
31–42	9
43–56	10
57–72	11
73–90	12
91–110	13
111–132	14
133–156	15
157–182	16
183–210	17
211–240	18

Example 4.1   Using the SMOG Readability Formula

Ten sentences from the beginning:

Living on the streets is often a vicious cycle of <u>addiction</u> and <u>homelessness</u>. People from all walks of life end up on the streets, sleeping outside in all kinds of weather. Most shelters will not accept an <u>intoxicated</u> person. Our program offers hope to homeless addicts. Every day, more than <u>200 individuals</u> wake up in one of our shelter <u>facilities</u>. Some will return to the street. Others will choose a path that <u>ultimately</u> returns them to their former lives. Each night there are <u>200</u> beds <u>available</u> at our men's and women's <u>facilities</u>. Here homeless users of <u>alcohol</u> or other drugs can rest and receive food and clothing. They can also see an <u>alternative</u> to the lives they are living. They see people underlined participating in our program who are on their way to underlined recovery. When addicts see their peers working, underlined studying, and staying sober, they see that they have a chance for underlined sobriety and a return to a healthy, underlined productive life. [17 words with three or more syllables]

Ten sentences from the middle:

The men's overnight emergency shelter has 36 beds available. The women's facility has ten overnight emergency beds. The shelters are open seven days a week on a first-come, first-served basis. We do not turn away people who are intoxicated. In the shelter they can shower, eat a healthy meal and receive clean clothes. They can sleep in a safe, warm bed. At this stage, we do not promise a bed or require participation. In order to receive any assistance beyond basic food, shelter, and clothing, the person must make a commitment to sobriety. If shelter guests want to get into the program, they must attend classes in order to be guaranteed a bed. Those who want to work toward underlined sobriety move into the first stage of the program where they learn about the disease of underlined addiction. [15 words with three or more syllables]

Ten sentences from the end:

underlined Residents who remain in the program underlined develop a lifestyle and underlined understanding about how that will support underlined ongoing sobriety. We provide resources to help them move back into underlined society. We offer underlined assistance with underlined employment, legal issues, and finding underlined independent housing. underlined Residents will stay in this underlined transitional program for 3 to 9 months underlined depending on how underlined extensive their needs are. They may underlined volunteer to teach classes in exchange for free room and board. As they move toward the final stage of underlined sobriety, there are underlined significant changes in their underlined responsibilities and underlined privileges. They are allowed to leave the facility during the day and on underlined overnight passes. underlined However, they must sign in and out when they visit the underlined facility where people are sobering up. The underlined interaction between residents who are underlined preparing to move back into underlined society and those just coming off the streets underlined reinforces the changes that program underlined participants have made in their lives. They, in turn, provide an underlined example to others. [27 words with three or more syllables]

Result: There is a total of 59 words with three or more syllables. The material is at the eleventh grade reading level.

The original SMOG Readability Formula was developed for use with documents that had thirty or more sentences. It is possible to use SMOG on passages with fewer than thirty sentences. If you have no other means to measure reading grade level, the formula and conversion table in figure 4.2 are useful for providing an approximate reading level. Just be aware that the conversions may not be as accurate because the norm was defined using thirty-sentence samples (McLaughlin, n.d.). Our stance is that a slightly inaccurate, ballpark reading level is better than no estimate at all. Unless you're a whiz at multiplication, you will need a calculator to use the formula for fewer than thirty sentences. Figure 4.2 demonstrates the use of the SMOG Readability Formula on a passage with fewer than thirty sentences. As we did on the longer sample, we underlined the words with three or more syllables.

Figure 4.2	SMOG Formula for Fewer than Thirty Sentences

Step 1: Count the total number of sentences.

Step 2: Count the number of words with three or more syllables in those sentences.

Step 3: Use the SMOG Conversion Table for Fewer than Thirty Sentences to locate the number of sentences in your document.

Step 4: Multiply the number of words with three or more syllables by the conversion number across from it. Use this number as the word count to determine the corresponding grade level in the SMOG Conversion Table (figure 4.1).

SMOG Conversion Table for Fewer than Thirty Sentences

Total Number of Sentences	Conversion Number
29	1.03
28	1.07
27	1.1
26	1.15
25	1.2
24	1.25
23	1.3

22	1.36
21	1.43
20	1.5
19	1.58
18	1.67
17	1.76
16	1.87
15	2.0
14	2.14
13	2.3
12	2.5
11	2.7
10	3

Example 4.2   Using SMOG on Fewer than Thirty Sentences

Does your child need after-school tutoring? Our program can help your child be successful at school. We offer free tutoring for elementary age children during the school year. Our program serves children ages six through 17. Volunteer tutors help students with math, English, and social studies. Tutoring is available Monday through Friday from 3:00 p.m. to 6:00 p.m. We provide a safe, supervised after-school environment. We also provide snacks and recreational activities. To qualify for our program, children must be eligible for free or reduced-price lunches at their school. If you would like more information or an application form, please call or email us. [19 words with three or more syllables]

Result: There are ten sentences in example 4.2. Using the *SMOG Conversion Table for Fewer than 30 Sentences*, we multiplied the 19 words with three or more syllables by three, which gave us a total score of 57. Referring back to the SMOG Conversion Table in figure 4.2, we can see that a score of 57 falls at the 11th grade reading level.

Now that you have the tools to calculate reading levels, you may be wondering what reading levels to aim for. As we noted in chapter 1, the average reading level for American adults is ninth grade; approximately one in seven Americans does not have a high school diploma, and nearly 30 percent have only a high school diploma or a GED (US Department of Education Institute of Education Sciences, 2003). We can expect many of these individuals to read four to five grade levels below the highest grade they report having completed in school (Arnold et al., 2006; Doak et al., 1996; National Work Group on Literacy and Health, 1998). People whose skills fall into the lowest category of functional literacy read at approximately the fifth grade level (Doak et al., 1996). How reading levels are generally classified is shown in table 4.1 (McGee, 2010).

Table 4.1	Classification of Reading Levels
Reading Level	**Classification**
fourth, fifth, sixth	easy
seventh, eighth	average difficulty
ninth	average or difficult depending on readers' familiarity with the content
tenth	difficult

The classifications shown in table 4.1 are estimates of reading difficulty. We cannot stress enough that a low reading level by itself does not guarantee readability. With that in mind, you can see that easy-to-read means keeping the materials you provide to clients at a level no higher than the sixth grade reading level.

CHOOSING AND USING ILLUSTRATIONS

Combining visuals with text is especially helpful for readers with limited literacy skills (Houts, Doak, Doak, & Loscalzo, 2006; Michielutte, Bahnson, Dignan, & Schroeder, 1992; Shriver, 1997). Pictures are not a substitute for clearly written text, but carefully chosen illustrations can motivate readers and help them interpret words. Ideally, illustrations and text reinforce each other. The graphics should help explain the meaning of the words and the words should help explain the meaning of the graphics. This means visuals should be placed close to the text they are intended to illustrate. If they are not, they will force readers to split their attention between the words and the graphic. This is particularly problematic for poor readers and makes it more difficult for them to grasp your message.

Poorly chosen illustrations will confuse readers and interfere with comprehension. If you have clip art or photographs available, it can be tempting to use them to decorate a brochure. However, using graphics as decoration or just because you have access to them is a bad idea. Instead of contributing to readers' comprehension, they will reduce it by diverting their attention from the text.

Types of Illustrations

Research indicates that the best illustrations are simple, realistic line drawings (Doak et al., 1996; Weiner et al., 2004). Photographs are acceptable as long as they do not contain a lot of background detail. Photographs with a great deal of background detail can be counterproductive because poor readers may be distracted by the pictures and pay less attention to the text. It's also best to avoid cartoon drawings or stick figures, which some people may not understand or take seriously (Centers for Disease Control and Prevention, 2009; Houts et al., 2006).

Options for Finding Illustrations

If your agency has the funds to hire a graphic artist, you can work with the artist to design the images you wish to project. This is, however, an expensive enterprise. Another option is to find an agency volunteer or board member who has the necessary time and talent to create graphic art or who can take appropriate photographs. If these options are not available to you, you may be able to find photos or clip art on the Internet. We do caution you that most of the free images we have seen on the Internet do not depict people, places, or backgrounds that are suitable for enhancing the readability of human service agency materials.

Cultural Appropriateness

If you are using images of people to illustrate agency materials, they should be representative of your target population in ethnicity, culture, age, class, and gender. Images of people who look like your audience convey that the information is meant for them and will encourage them to look at your materials. This is especially important if you use images of people on the front cover of a brochure. If you are trying to reach a diverse audience, use images that show the diversity that exists among your agency's clients.

If you are using images of homes, neighborhoods, schools, or houses of worship, be sure they resemble those your target audience is familiar with. Compare the cover illustration in figure 4.3 with the one in figure 4.4. Figure 4.3 was a graphic artist's initial sketch for the cover of a brochure targeting low-income families with at-risk children. A low-income inner-city or rural parent might well look at the people and the background in

Figure 4.3 Inappropriate Illustration for Low-Income Target Audience

Figure 4.4 Appropriate Illustration for Low-Income Target Audience

this illustration and think, "This information is not meant for me and my family." Even without the background, the people are more formally dressed and posed than most ordinary people. The illustration in figure 4.4 features a family that is casually dressed without a lot of distracting background. They are sitting at a kitchen table, something most people have in their homes.

BROCHURE FORMATS

Many human service agencies produce or distribute tri-fold or three-panel brochures. The problem with this format is that it may not be obvious to readers with limited literacy skills where to begin reading or which information is most important. A traditional tri-fold brochure is printed on both sides of a standard 8½-by-11-inch sheet of paper. The right panel is folded over the

Figure 4.5 Traditional Tri-Fold Brochure

center panel and the left panel is then folded over the right to become the cover, as shown in figure 4.5. To open the brochure, the reader unfolds the outside front panel which uncovers the first inside panel and one back panel. Herein lies a potential problem. It may not be obvious to readers with limited literacy skills what to read first. If they open it all the way, they will see all three inside panels. If they do not immediately unfold the right panel they will not see the remaining two inside panels. If they are not motivated to open it completely, they may miss important content.

One way to guide readers is to number the inside panels 1, 2, 3 at the top. All the need-to-know information should be on the three inside panels because many people will not turn the brochure over to read the content on the back. If you choose to print anything on the back panels, it should be only nice-to-know information such as your agency's mission statement or the names of your board of directors or community partners.

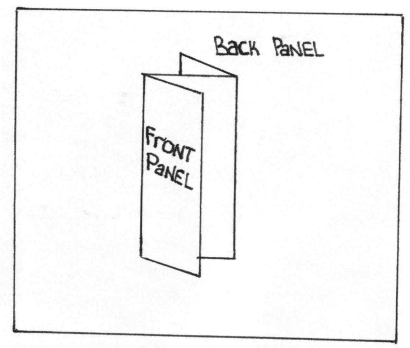

Figure 4.6 Accordion or Z-Fold Brochure

The accordion or Z-fold, shown in figure 4.6, is another three-panel option. This format is not good for poor readers because when fully opened, they see only two inside panels with content. If you have more than two panels' worth of need-to-know content, readers would have to turn it over and read the back, which many will not do. This is especially true for those with limited literacy skills.

A half-fold or book-style brochure, shown in figure 4.7, is also printed on standard 8½-by-11-inch stock. It eliminates the reader's dilemma of which panel to read first, thus it is particularly well-suited for readers with limited literacy skills. It is our first choice when we are creating a brochure for people with limited literacy skills. The reader reads the cover, opens the brochure, and reads the two inside panels. As with the tri-fold formats, do not put any critical information on the back panel because many people will never look at the back of the brochure.

Figure 4.7 Half-Fold Brochure

EVALUATING OVERALL APPROPRIATENESS FOR READERS
WITH LIMITED LITERACY SKILLS

As you now know, readability includes much more than reading level. As discussed in chapter 3, you begin the process of creating readable materials by defining your purpose and your target audience. These steps will help you limit the content to what your audience needs to know for the piece to accomplish its purpose. Using a readability checklist will help you assess overall appropriateness for audiences with limited literacy skills.

The readability checklist in figure 4.8 incorporates the guidelines for readability we provided in chapter 1. You can use it as a tool to assess the overall readability of your agency's print materials. We suggest that you begin by using the checklist to assess the materials your agency currently provides to clients. The results will indicate which materials could benefit from revision and what types of changes in format, content, and graphics would improve their readability. Once you have made your revisions, you can apply the checklist a second time to be sure that the format and content are consistent with the guidelines for readability. You can also use the checklist to fine-tune any new materials you develop. Once you have completed a first draft, the checklist will help you pinpoint elements in need of revision.

Figure 4.8   **Readability Checklist**

Mark the reading grade level below.

☐ 4th grade   ☐ 5th grade   ☐ 6th grade (easy)

☐ 7th grade   ☐ 8th grade (average)

☐ 9th grade (average or difficult depending on readers' familiarity with the content)

☐ 10th grade or higher (difficult)

Format	Throughout	In some places	Rarely/Never
No words in all caps			
Left margins even; right margins ragged; text is not centered			
Important points underlined, boldface, or surrounded by white space			
No italics or fancy fonts			
Text in short blocks with white space before and after			
Serif fonts used			
No type smaller than 12 points			

Content	Throughout	In some places	Rarely/Never
Definitions of or examples for unfamiliar words			
Titles and headings to guide readers			
One idea per paragraph			
Short words			
Short sentences			
Conversational style of writing			
No contractions			
No tables, charts, or graphs			
No colons or semicolons			
No roman numerals			

Graphics	All	Some	None	n/a
Illustrations are close to text they illustrate				
Illustrations are related to text they are meant to illustrate				
Images of people resemble the target audience				
Illustrations are without distracting background details				

The tools in this chapter will enable you to evaluate the reading levels and overall readability of any agency materials you create or revise. Once you are satisfied with the reading level, content, and format of your material, you will be ready to for the next step: conducting learner verification interviews to assess how well your intended audience comprehends the messages you wish to convey.

REFERENCES

Arnold, C. L., Davis, T. C., Frempong, J. O., Humiston, S. G., Bocchini, A., Kennen, E. M., & Lloyd-Puryear, M. (2006). Assessment of newborn screening parent education materials. *Pediatrics*, *117*(5), S320–S325.

Centers for Disease Control and Prevention. (2009). *Simply put: A guide for creating easy-to-understand materials* (3rd ed.). Retrieved from http://www.cdc.gov/healthliteracy/pdf/simply_put.pdf.

Doak, C. C., Doak, L. G., & Root, J. (1996). *Teaching patients with low literacy skills* (2nd ed.). Philadelphia, PA: Lippincott. Online: http://www.hsph.harvard.edu/healthliteracy/resources/teaching-patients-with-low-literacy-skills/.

Fitzsimmons, P. R., Michael, B. D., Hulley, J. L., & Scott, G. O. (2010). A readability assessment of online Parkinson's disease information. *Journal of the Royal College of Physicians of Edinburgh, 40,* 292–296. doi: 10.4997/JRCPE.2010.401.

Houts, P., Doak, C., Doak, L., & Loscalzo, M. (2006). The role of pictures in improving health communication: A review of research on attention, comprehension, recall, and adherence. *Patient Education and Counseling, 61*(2), 173–190. doi: 10.1016/j.pec.2005.05.004.

McGee, J. (2010). *Toolkit for making written material clear and effective.* Retrieved from http://www.cms.gov/Outreach-and-Education/Outreach/WrittenMaterialsToolkit/index.html.

McLaughlin, G. H. (1974). Temptations of the Flesch. *Instructional Science, 2,* 367–385.

McLaughlin, G. H. (n.d.). *SMOG: Simple Measure of Gobbledygook.* Retrieved from http://webpages.charter.net/ghal/SMOG.htm.

Michielutte, R., Bahnson, J., Dignan, M. R., & Schroeder, E. M. (1992). The use of illustrations and narrative text style to improve readability of a health education brochure. *Journal of Cancer Education, 7*(3), 251–260. doi: 10.1080/08858199209528176.

National Work Group on Literacy and Health. (1998). Communicating with patients who have limited literacy skills. Report of the National Work Group on Literacy and Health. *Journal of Family Practice, 46,* 168–176.

Shriver, K. A. (1997). *Dynamics in document design.* New York, NY: John Wiley.

US Department of Education Institute of Education Sciences. (2003). *National Assessment of Adult Literacy (NAAL).* Retrieved from http://nces.ed.gov/naal/.

Weiner, J., Aguirre, A., Ravenell, K.,
    Kovath, K., McDevit, L., Murphy, J.,
    . . . Shea, J. A. (2004). Designing an
    illustrated patient satisfaction instru-
    ment for low-literacy populations.
    *American Journal of Managed Care,
    10*(11), 853–860.

Collecting and Using Feedback

Have a look at your prospective readers. Talk to them. Find out what they know, what they don't know, and what they want to know.

—**R. F. Flesch,** *The Art of Readable Writing*

Collecting and using feedback from your intended audience could make the difference between creating materials your clients read and act upon and creating materials that they ignore or throw away as soon as you are out of sight. Pretesting is the process that enables you to collect feedback from your target audience and use it to make revisions. It is the best way to learn if your prospective readers find your messages clear, meaningful, and culturally appropriate. Unfortunately, this step is often ignored when agencies develop new materials.

If your agency produces pamphlets, brochures, flyers, or booklets to give to clients, those clients are the best people to tell you whether your messages are clear and your materials appealing. If you provide your clientele with printed eligibility information, rules, policies, or any other information meant to benefit them, only they can tell you whether they understand that information. Pretesting means showing your materials to individuals representative of your target audience and asking them specific questions about their responses and opinions. Pretesting is particularly important when you are developing materials for audiences with limited literacy skills because the results can tell you whether your intended audience gets your message. You can pretest the content of any materials designed with clients in mind:

pamphlets, brochures, flyers, fact sheets, rules, application forms, eligibility criteria, and even posters.

Pretesting will let you know if you have inadvertently assumed that your readers have more knowledge than they actually have. Information and language that you take for granted may be incomprehensible to your target audience, especially if they lack prior knowledge about the topic. You may recall, from our discussion of the process of reading in chapter 1, that readers' prior knowledge provides a foundation that can help them make sense of new information. Be careful that your own prior knowledge does not end up preventing your readers from making sense of your messages.

In addition to helping you improve the clarity of your materials, pretesting provides you with information on how your audience views the appropriateness, appeal, and general acceptability of your material. Pretesting allows you to hear directly from the target audience and enables you to make specific revisions in your materials before you print a final version. It does not guarantee a perfect product, but well-designed pretest questions can help you avoid giving your audience messages that are unclear or incomprehensible. Pretesting requires five basic steps:

1. Identify your target audience
2. Identify the purpose of the material
3. Identify the key points
4. Develop interview questions
5. Find representatives of your target audience

You do not need to interview large numbers of people. As few as ten people can provide you with valuable feedback on the clarity of your messages and the attractiveness and cultural appropriateness of the material (Doak, Doak, & Root, 1996). From a cost-benefit standpoint, investing a bit of time before you print final versions of your materials may save you from expending time, effort, and energy to produce materials your intended audience cannot or will not read. The effort you put into creating readable materials is worthwhile only if your target audience sees them as potentially interesting and meaningful enough to read. You have accomplished nothing if they throw away your materials as soon as they walk out of your office.

Although you can get useful information from as few as ten people, be aware that if your materials are aimed at a culturally diverse audience, it is important to pretest with several representatives from each group you are trying to reach. If you do not do this, you could miss elements in your materials that are culturally inappropriate, offensive, or just plain mystifying to some segments of your audience.

HOW TO DEVELOP A PRETEST

Step 1: identify the target audience and define the purpose of the material. In chapter 3 we discussed the importance of identifying the target audience and defining the purpose of any materials you develop. Before you create questions for a pretest, you should be able to clearly state who you want to reach and what you want them to know or be able to do after they read the material.

Step 2: list the key points. In addition to identifying the purpose or objectives, you should identify the key points in the material. The key points are the specific information readers need to know in order for the material to accomplish its purpose.

Step 3: develop pretest questions. Once you have identified the target audience, defined your purpose, and listed the key points in the material, you are ready to develop questions for your pretest. Your pretest questions should be designed to tell you whether people understand the overall message and the words you have used, and if they find the material attractive and relevant to their lives. The information you collect will help you determine what is effective and what you may want to change to make your materials clearer or more acceptable to your target audience. To get this information, you will need a mix of closed-ended and open-ended questions.

Closed-Ended Questions

Use closed-ended questions to gather basic information:

- Would you pick up this brochure?
- Do the people on the front of the booklet look like people you know?

You can also use closed-ended questions to get specific information:

- Who do you think would be interested in the information in this brochure?

It is important to word your questions as neutrally as possible. Try to avoid leading questions that suggest you are looking for specific answers, for example: "Do you think the information in this pamphlet is helpful?" or "Do you like the pictures in the brochure?" Leading questions will prompt some people to try to please the interviewer by answering yes.

Open-Ended Questions

Open-ended questions allow the individuals you interview to express their opinions and to comment on aspects of your materials that you might not have considered. The best way to formulate open-ended questions is to begin with the words *what* or *how* or with expressions such as "tell me about" or "describe." For example, you can ask, "How do you think people might use the information in this pamphlet?" or "What do you think about the pictures in the brochure?"

Combining Closed-Ended and Open-Ended Questions

To get useful information, you will need a combination of closed-ended and open-ended questions. For example, you might ask, "Would you pick this pamphlet up?" You would follow up a yes answer with "What would make you want to pick it up?" For someone who said no, you could ask, "What is it about the flyer that would make you not want to pick it up?" or "What could we change that would make you want to pick it up?" Asking open-ended follow-up questions that prompt respondents to explain their reasons for answering yes or no to specific questions will help you figure out what you may need to change to improve the overall readability and appeal of your materials.

We do caution you to be careful about beginning questions with the word *why*, particularly when you're asking for an explanation of a negative answer. For example, asking people "Why wouldn't you pick this up?" can sound as though you are challenging them to defend their answers. You can soften why questions by using phrases such as "can you tell me why" or "help me understand why" in your follow-up questions.

Structuring the Questions

It's best to begin a pretest questionnaire with a general question, such as, "Tell me what this brochure is about" or "What do you think this flyer is about?" If your material contains suggestions, advice, or instructions, you would want find out if respondents comprehend what it is asking them to do. You would also want to know whether they would be likely to follow any of the suggestions, and what might make it easier or more likely for them to do so. You can begin with a general question, such as, "What is this brochure asking people to do?" You can then follow up by asking more specific questions: "Would you do what it asks you to do?" and "Would other people you know do what it asks you to do?" As discussed earlier, asking follow-up questions after positive and negative responses will help you determine what you could change that might motivate people to act on the information.

If you are pretesting material such as an application form or rules for a residential care facility, your questions should be designed to determine if people understand the individual items. This means you will need to ask respondents to tell you in their own words what various items mean or are asking them to do.

Asking about Illustrations

If your material contains illustrations, it is important to ask respondents for their reactions to the graphics. This could include questions such as:

- What do you think of these pictures?
- What do you think the people in the picture(s) are doing?
- Do the people in the pictures look like people you know?

The answers to these questions will help you fine-tune your illustrations. We learned this firsthand when we asked whether pictures of people in a fact sheet one of us developed "look like people you know." A number of our respondents said no. The answers to the follow-up question, "What can we do to make them look more like people you know?" told us the people in the drawings looked "too dressed up" to a number of our respondents. A few simple changes in the illustrations made the fact sheet more appealing to our target audience.

Questions for Culturally Diverse Audiences

If you are trying to reach culturally diverse audiences, you will want to know if the images, language, and content in your materials are culturally acceptable and familiar to your target audiences. When you get negative responses, it's important to ask follow-up questions to learn what changes would make the material more culturally acceptable. Examples of the kinds of questions you can ask include:

- Do the people in the pictures look like your family members and friends? If the answer is no, follow up by asking what changes would make them look more familiar.
- Are these the words you would use to describe . . . ? If the answer is no, follow up by asking what words they would use.
- Is this something the people in your community are likely to do? If the answer is no, ask them to help you understand why people would not do what the material suggests.
- "Would you or your family members use these services?" If the answer is no, follow up with an open-ended question such as, "What could we say that might motivate you and your family to use these services?"

HOW TO CONDUCT A PRETEST: AN EXAMPLE

We will use an educational handout one of us wrote to take you through the process of conducting a pretest. The target audience for the handout was low-income parents with limited literacy skills who were enrolled in a family literacy program. Most of the program's clients had grown up in homes with few or no books and parents who did not read to them when they were children. The goal of the family literacy program was to help its clients break the cycle of low literacy. The program provided the parents with tutoring to improve their literacy skills and literacy activities to do at home with their preschool children. The handout in figure 5.1 was designed to help the parents work with their children at home. Because we had no funds to include graphics, this piece had only text with no illustrations.

| Figure 5.1 | Family Literacy Parent Handout |

Helping Your Children Learn to Read and Write

What do children need to learn about letters and words when they begin to read and write?

- Words stand for things and ideas.
- Everything has a name that we can write.
- We read and write from left to right and top to bottom of the page.
- Words have spaces between them.
- Words are made up of letters
- There is a difference between letters and words.
- Letters have certain sounds in spoken words.

How do children learn that printed letters and words have meaning?

Seeing lots of print at home helps children learn that printed words have meanings. Reading picture books helps children learn that print has meaning. Seeing printed signs and labels helps too.

Why do children need to understand that printed letters and words have meaning?

Very young children think the pictures in books tell the stories. They may not know that you are reading the print, not the pictures. As children learn to read, they begin to understand that print tells us things pictures cannot tell us.

What if my children write their letters and words wrong?

Children may not make all their letters correctly at first. Do not worry or get upset if they make mistakes. Just praise them and give them lots of hugs and smiles for trying to write.

- Do not worry if some letters are backward or have pieces missing.
- Do not worry if they write backward or from the bottom of the page to the top. Many children do this at first.
- Do not worry if they have trouble with spelling. They will learn to spell as they get older.

How can I help my children learn to read and write?
Here are some things you can do:

1. Write signs to label things in your home. For example, table, chair, stove, bed, TV, door, window, floor, wall, and so on. Ask your children to tape the signs on the things they stand for.

2. Make a name card for each person in the family. Let your children make the cards if they can. If not, help them write each name.

3. Ask your children to help you make a list before you go grocery shopping. If they know their letters, you can spell the words for them. You can also let them use their own spelling. Do this on a day when you are not in a hurry. It can take a while!

4. Save soap wrappers, the fronts of cereal boxes, cans, or other containers. Take them when you and your children go shopping. Help your children find the product that is the same as the sample.

5. Make a "My Very Own Words" list. Ask your children to name some of their favorite words. These might be words like Mommy, Daddy, Grandma, ice cream, birthday, and toy. Help them write each word on a card. At first, it may help if they draw a picture to go with each word or if you cut pictures from magazines. Keep the cards in a box or plastic baggie. Once a week or so, get them out. See how many of the words your children can read.

6. Point at and read out loud words and labels on food containers and road signs, in restaurants, and other places. Doing this every day will help your children learn that print has meaning.

Step 1 is to identify the target audience and purpose. The target audience for the handout in figure 5.1 was parents of preschool-age children. The purpose of the piece was to enable the parents to:

1. Provide their children with a variety of age-appropriate print materials at home
2. Help their children develop beginning reading and writing skills

Step 2 is to identify the key points. There are three key points in this piece:

1. Children need to see lots of print in the home to learn that print has meaning.
2. Parents should encourage children's attempts to write and not worry about them writing correctly.
3. Parents can do simple reading and writing activities with their children to help them recognize letters and words.

Step 3 is to prepare the pretest questions. Figure 5.2 shows the pretest questionnaire for the parent handout. As you can see, it uses a combination of open-ended and closed-ended questions to gather specific information about the material we were pretesting. Although it is brief, it provided us with feedback that enabled us to make the handout clearer before printing the final version.

Figure 5.2	**Sample Pretest Questionnaire**

Pretest Questionnaire for "Helping Your Children Learn to Read and Write"

After respondents read the material, allow them to keep the handout while you ask the questions.

1. What are some things you can do at home to help your child learn what letters and words mean?
2. What should you do if your child writes letters or words incorrectly?
3. Which words in this piece are hard to understand?
4. What could we do to make this material easier to understand?
5. Which of the activities do you think you would do with your children?
   □ 1 □ 2 □ 3 □ 4 □ 5 □ 6 (check all that apply)
   Probe (ask about each checked item individually and record the answers): Tell me why you would do this.

6. Which of the activities do you think you would not do?

☐ 1 ☐ 2 ☐ 3 ☐ 4 ☐ 5 ☐ 6 (check all that apply)

Probe (ask about each checked item individually and record the answers): Tell me why you would not do this.

7. What more could this handout tell you that would help you to do the activities?

8. Do you think other parents you know would be willing to do some of these activities?

Probe: Why or why not?

PLANNING YOUR PRETEST

We realize that some agencies may not have the time or the resources for pretesting. However, for those who do, we are providing detailed instructions for planning and carrying out a pretest. These are instructions we wish we had had when we conducted our first pretest.

Finding Representatives of Your Target Audience

You will need to pretest your materials with individuals who are part of your target audience. If you are developing materials specific to your agency and its services, the most obvious place to find representatives of your target audience is in your own office or your agency's waiting room. We have also successfully pretested materials in clients' homes during home visits. Other possible venues include:

- community sites such as churches, senior centers, and food pantries
- adult basic education or GED classes
- waiting areas in Social Security offices, public social service agencies, WIC centers, job training centers

If you are producing educational materials aimed at members of the general public (e.g., on child abuse, domestic violence, mental health, specific disabilities, or other such topics), the locations suggested above may also be useful. For materials such as rules and regulations in a residential care facility, you may be able to enlist volunteers from within your temporarily captive audience. While we do not think it advisable (or ethical) to require residents to be interviewed, some may be willing if you present the pretest as a way for them to help others better understand the facility's rules.

If you want to pretest outside your own agency, you must, of course, request permission ahead of time from the agency. Seeking permission has the added benefit of allowing you to explain why you are asking to pretest your materials and thus spreading the word about what you are doing and the importance of readability.

Who Should Conduct the Pretests?

If you developed the materials, you are the best person to conduct the pretest interviews because you will presumably be making the revisions. There is no substitute for hearing firsthand what respondents say, observing their nonverbal communication, and noting their responses. Do not give up, however, if you cannot do it yourself. The next best thing is to enlist other agency staff, volunteers, or students to do it.

Low-tech versus High-tech Questionnaires

You can use paper or electronic questionnaires. The advantage of paper questionnaires is that they require no advance preparation. All you need are enough copies for the interviews. The disadvantage is that in order to easily review and tabulate the responses someone will have to transcribe them into a word-processing program.

Recording respondents' answers directly on a laptop will enable you to tabulate the data without any additional transcription. To do this, you must first create a master copy of your questionnaire in an electronic format. You can use standard word-processing software to create this document or software that creates forms that limit input to specific answer fields, such as Adobe portable document format (PDF) files. You will need a separate form on which to record each respondent's answers, and you must make sure that whoever conducts interviews has the appropriate software on their laptops.

Training the Pretest Interviewers

It is important to do some advance preparation before you conduct your pretest interviews. You can adapt the sample materials we have provided to plan and conduct a brief training for pretest interviewers. These materials will also help you prepare yourself if you are going to conduct the pretest interviews yourself. You will need a packet for each interviewer that contains:

- an explanation of the purpose of the materials and who the target audience is (see figure 5.3)
- an interview's guide (see figure 5.4)
- an interviewer information form (see figure 5.5)
- your pretest questionnaire
- copies of the material to be pretested

Ideally, you will be able to pretest a version of your material that includes any illustrations you intend to use. A photocopied version is fine. Be sure to review everything in the packet with the interviewers. If you are using several interviewers, you may want to have them pair up for mock interviews as part of the training. Practicing will make them more comfortable with the process and will give them a chance to ask any questions that arise before they conduct the real pretest interviews. The sample interviewer training introduction in figure 5.3 includes basic information for the interviewers. Providing this information is especially important if your interviewers are not familiar with the rationale for creating easy-to-read materials. You can adapt the introduction to your needs depending on the type and purpose of the material you are pretesting.

Figure 5.3	Sample Interviewer Training Introduction

Background

We are pretesting our new easy-to-read material by interviewing the people to whom we intend to give it. Pretesting will help us learn what we can do to improve the material. You have a packet with copies of the material and questions we would like you to ask the people you interview. With your help, we will be able to interview people in our community who are members of our target audience. The information you collect will help us revise the material to make it clearer and more appealing to our target audience.

The pretest results are intended to answer these questions:

1. Is the material attractive to the audience we are targeting? If it doesn't appeal to them, they won't pick it up from a pamphlet rack or table or read it if we give it to them.

2. Does our target audience understand what we are trying to say? People with limited literacy skills have fewer sources for information than people with more sophisticated literacy skills. If the message isn't clear or confuses them, we haven't done our job.

3. Is there anything about the message or the format that is offensive or inappropriate for our audience? Is there anything that annoys them or that detracts from the message we are trying to get across?

4. Is our message persuasive? Are they likely to comply with any actions we suggest? Is there any way we could make our message more persuasive and increase the likelihood they would follow our suggestions?

The Interviewer's Role

We have developed a series of questions for you to ask. It is very important that every interviewer ask the questions on the questionnaire in the order they appear and exactly as they are written. Collecting the same information in the same way will help us determine what we need to revise to improve the material before we print it.

The interviewer's guide in figure 5.4 will be helpful if you are planning to conduct pretest interviews yourself or if you are training others to do the interviews. The instructions in the guide are meant to ensure that the interviewer appears objective and encourages respondents to express their honest opinions and that anyone who conducts interviews asks the questions in the same order and in the same way for every interview. For your results to be meaningful, it is important that anyone who conducts pretest interviews follows the guide.

Figure 5.4	Sample Interviewer's Guide

Interviewer's Guide

General tips

1. Put respondents at ease by being friendly and actively listening. This means using eye contact, smiling when appropriate, assuming an open physical posture, and responding to comments with neutral probes such as "tell me more" or "can you tell me what you mean by that?"

2. Bring something you can read while respondents are reading the material. If you watch them read, they may feel uncomfortable or try to hurry in order not to keep you waiting. If they have children with them, you might want to talk with the children while the parent is reading.

Conducting the interview

1. Use the following introduction with each potential respondent:

   "Hello, my name is _____. I'd like to show you a [brochure, flyer, booklet, etc.] that our agency is developing. The people who put it together asked me to help them find out what people think of it and if it's easy to understand. They want this information so they can make changes that will make it better. I wasn't involved in putting this together, so I won't be offended by anything you say. I'll give it to you to read, and when you're done, I'll ask you some questions. I'll write down the answers you give me, but I will not write down your name. No one will know that these are your answers."

2. Give the interviewee a copy of the material. Explain that what you're showing them is not the final version. People usually respond positively when you tell them you want their feedback in order to improve the materials your agency provides. Tell the person that you are testing the materials to see how easy it is for people to understand. State very clearly that you are not testing them, you are testing the material.

3. Ask the interviewee to read the material. Tell them they can take as much time as they need to read it.

4. After they read the material, allow them to keep it in hand while they answer the questions. You want them to be able to refer back to it as you ask your questions. Tell them: "I'd like to ask you some questions now. We want to see if

the material is clearly written and to see how you feel about it. There are no right or wrong answers to the questions I'm going to ask you. It's fine if you want to look at the material while you're answering the questions."

5. Ask the questions exactly as they are written on the questionnaire and in the order they appear. This will ensure consistency among all interviews.

6. Try not to prompt respondents if they have difficulty expressing themselves. Give them time to try to explain what they mean.

7. Record exactly what respondents say without trying to interpret it. The words they use may suggest ways to communicate more effectively with the target audience.

8. Try not to interrupt the interview to answer questions. Write any questions people ask on the form; if several people ask the same question, it may indicate something we need to clarify. Tell respondents you will try to answer their questions when you're done with the interview and try to bring the focus back to the material being tested.

9. Gently direct respondents' attention back to the material if they start telling you a story of their own or a relative's experience related to the material.

10. Try to clarify any answers you don't understand by asking, "Can you tell me what you mean by that?" or "Please tell me more about that." Write down exactly what they say.

11. Be as neutral as you can. Do not give nonverbal encouragement by nodding your head or making comments such as "that's right" or "good answer." If a respondent asks if an answer is correct, explain that there are no right or wrong answers and that what you want to know is whether the material is clear and makes sense to them.

If you are not doing the interviews yourself, we suggest that you provide interviewers with an interviewer identification form similar to the one in figure 5.5. It is helpful if you need to contact them for any reason after the interviews. We always include space for comments. Interviewers' observations of people's verbal and nonverbal reactions to the material can help you identify problem areas, and having their contact information gives you a way to get in touch with them if you want to discuss or ask them questions about their comments. These comments can also help you identify any problematic questions on your questionnaire that you might want to revise for clarity.

Figure 5.5	Sample Interviewer Identification Form

Interviewer Identification Form

Thank you very much for helping us pretest our materials. Please complete the following and return it with your completed questionnaires.

Name _____

Address _____

_____

Telephone _____

E-mail address _____

Please write below any comments, observations, or suggestions that might help us improve the questionnaire or the materials.

_____

_____

_____

USING PRETEST RESULTS TO REVISE YOUR MATERIALS

Once you have conducted your interviews, you will need to tabulate your results. This means organizing and recording all the responses to each question so that you can see at a glance the range of responses. The answers should give you a sense of what is clear and what is not, as well as how attractive the piece is to your audience. If you learn that the majority of your respondents could not understand the message, found the piece unattractive or unappealing, or indicated it was culturally inappropriate, you will have to determine whether your best option is to make major revisions or to begin again from scratch (National Cancer Institute, 2003).

If respondents raise a few concerns, your decisions about what and whether to revise depend on how many people you included in the pretest and what kinds of issues they raised. When you pretest with a small number of people (e.g., ten or twelve), the National Cancer Institute (2003) advises taking their concerns seriously. This is especially important if the concerns involve problems with understanding key concepts or cultural acceptability (Doak et al., 1996). If respondents had difficulty comprehending the information, it should prompt you to revise the content to make it clearer. If respondents found any content, language, or images culturally unacceptable, their responses will help you improve those elements.

REFERENCES

Doak, C. C., Doak, L. G., & Root, J. (1996). *Teaching patients with low literacy skills* (2nd ed.). Philadelphia, PA: Lippincott. Available online: http://www.hsph.harvard.edu/health literacy/resources/doak-book/index .html.

Flesch, R. F. (1974). *The art of readable writing* (25th anniversary ed.). New York, NY: Collier Books.

National Cancer Institute. (2003). *Clear and simple: Effective print materials for low-literate readers.* Retrieved from http://www.cancer.gov/cancer topics/cancerlibrary/clear-and-simple/.

Writing for Every Agency Audience

The single biggest problem in communication is the illusion that it has taken place.

—**George Bernard Shaw**

It isn't only clients who will benefit if your agency incorporates the principles of readability into all of its materials and communications. If you use print to communicate with volunteers, donors, board members, colleagues, the media, or the general public, spelling and grammatical errors can contribute to a suspicion of less than competent performance. Those you are trying to reach may set aside communications filled with fancy language and long convoluted sentences because they take too long to read. Using passive voice may leave readers wondering who did what or unsure of how you want them to respond. And, of course, none of your audiences will react positively if they have to put a lot of effort into trying to understand the information you provide.

Perhaps you have, in the past, been frustrated by uninvolved board members, unenthusiastic volunteers, or unresponsive donors or disappointed in the media's coverage of your agency's activities. It's possible that ineffective or unclear communication played a role in these situations. Although our focus so far has been on communicating with clients, the techniques and guidelines that increase readability can also improve your ability to communicate effectively with all of your agency's audiences: boards of directors, other community agencies, donors, volunteers, employees, and media contacts. Every one of these audiences needs clear messages from you in order to fulfill their roles.

When you are writing messages for constituencies other than clients, the basic questions we introduced in chapter 3 still apply. First, who is the audience? Members of a board of directors have different information and communication needs from partner agencies, representatives of the media, or the general public. Second, what is the purpose of the message? What do you want them to do? Do you want them to send money, to refer clients, to advocate for your programs, or to take some other specific action? Once you define the desired outcome, you can focus your message on what your audience needs to know and weed out any nice-to-know information that could distract from your message.

Finally, do not forget to provide your audience with a context for what you write. Don't assume that they know as much as you do about the topic or that they have enough background information to make sense of your message. How do you provide a context? By writing a short sentence or two that sets the stage for the message. Once you have done that, you can move directly into your message. Without setting the stage, you may come across as abrupt or you may confuse readers by assuming they know more than they do. As example 6.1 illustrates, what you want is a balance between brevity and detail; you want to offer enough context for clarity (i.e., what they *need* to know) without getting into extraneous (i.e., nice-to-know) details that will dilute your message and turn off or confuse your readers.

Example 6.1	**Setting the Stage for Your Message**
Setting the stage	The message
Happy Helpers, Inc., has had some recent staff changes. Neal Down has resigned and Hedda Haire is on maternity leave.	We urgently need volunteers to staff the front office for the next six weeks. Please contact the office if you can volunteer some extra time while we are short of staff.

COMMUNICATING WITH BOARDS OF DIRECTORS

Members of many nonprofit agencies' boards of directors represent a cross-section of community members. Boards often include professionals with different training and experience, individuals with a variety of racial, ethnic, and cultural backgrounds, and representatives of various interest groups in the community. What these individuals presumably have in common is that they support the agency's mission with their time and money even though most are not experts in what your agency does.

How does this relate to readability? Most organizations provide prospective board members with printed or electronic materials, in the form of board packets, as part of the recruitment process. These materials should clearly describe board members' roles and the agency's expectations for their participation. Your goal is to provide enough information for prospective board members to make an informed decision about joining your board. In our experience, individuals who join boards without a clear understanding of their roles and expectations often drop out or fail to participate actively.

Do not bury what prospective board members need to know in unnecessary details. Provide concise descriptions of your agency's mission, services, programs, and clientele, as well as funding sources and status. Give them clear explanations (in active voice!) of the time commitment, financial obligation, and any other expectations for board members. Direct them to your agency's website or a contact person if they have questions or want additional information.

Most board members are busy people, and once they're on board, streamlining the materials you send them is one way to display respect for their time. If you send out hard copy or electronic packets before board meetings, or any other time you give board members written materials, your goal should be to minimize the time and effort it takes to read them. How do you do this? By advocating that your agency avoid "the staff's temptation to send a ton of stuff, the better to inform and impress the board" (Masaoka, 2010, n.p.). This means being concise and using plain language to tell them what they need to know or what you want them to do. In our experience, most board members, ourselves included, skim through the information they receive from the agency. Your goal should be to do whatever you can to increase the chances that board members will read what you send and find it useful.

As board members ourselves, we have both, at times, received information that assumed a level of knowledge and understanding far beyond what we possessed. These experiences taught us how important it is to avoid using agency or professional jargon and acronyms when communicating with board members. Your board members may be a more educated audience than many of your clients, but that does not mean they will understand your agency language any better than your clients do. Expecting them to be familiar with jargon and acronyms, or assuming they have intimate knowledge of the complexities of agency operations, can confuse or even alienate them. Consider, too, that board members are ambassadors for your agency. When you provide them with clearly articulated explanations of the work your agency does, you are giving them the information they need to spread the word, effectively and accurately, among their social and professional networks about who you are and what you do.

When the time comes to request action from your board members, use plain language to tell them what you want them to do. Example 6.2 is a message sent to members of a human service agency's board of directors. The writer's intention was to request board members' assistance in contacting legislators to advocate for an agency program.

Example 6.2   **A Message to Agency Board Members**

Attention Board Members:

Funding cuts for prevention programs for at-risk youth are being considered by the DJA. These cuts are to be accompanied by increased funding for juvenile detention centers. It has been requested that representatives from Positive Youth Development meet with legislators to prevent what happened with Willie M in the 1980s. Evidence is to be provided that PYD is more cost-effective and has better outcomes than incarceration for young people at risk. Please let us know if you can help.

What's wrong with this message? Aside from the obvious use of acronyms, it assumes that board members are familiar with the agency's funding sources and history (i.e., "what happened with Willie M in the 1980s). Do you think that those who received this message would understand the situation or know what the sender was asking of them? We think not. We have rewritten the message in example 6.3 to clarify what the sender was trying to communicate.

Example 6.3   **Revised Message to Agency Board Members**

Attention Board Members:

We need your help. The funding for our Positive Youth Development program is at risk. The Department of Juvenile Affairs is considering cutting funds for gang prevention programs like ours and increasing funding for juvenile detention centers. We are asking board members to meet with legislators to explain how Positive Youth Development is more cost effective and has better outcomes than locking young people up. Please call Rhoda Dendron at 555-1212 for further information if you are available to meet with legislators on May 15.

The second message takes into consideration who the audience is and the outcome the sender wishes to accomplish. It makes a specific request. The message is clear because it avoids jargon and acronyms that might confuse readers, and it uses the active voice to explain the situation. Additionally, the rewritten message tells readers at the very beginning that the sender wants their help. At the end it tells them specifically how to volunteer that help.

COMMUNICATING WITH PROFESSIONALS AND AGENCIES IN YOUR COMMUNITY

When you communicate with other agencies or professionals who refer clients to you or serve the same population, readability can still be an issue. It is easy to assume that practitioners and agencies with whom you collaborate use the same jargon and acronyms that you do. However, it's quite possible that they do not speak your professional or agency language or are only vaguely familiar with it, thus they may not fully understand what you are trying to communicate. You have nothing to lose by incorporating the principles of readability into your communications with outside agencies and professionals. If you think about it, most of us are inundated with electronic and hard-copy messages every day. You probably appreciate receiving straightforward information that addresses only what is relevant to you. That is what you should be providing to others.

WRITING READABLE GRANT PROPOSALS

If you have written proposals for grants or contracts, you may have found that many public and private funding organizations do not follow the principles we have laid out for readable writing. Instructions from private foundations, corporate funders, and government agencies are sometimes convoluted and unclear, and completing applications and proposals can be a confusing and arduous process. What funders are asking you to tell them may not always be clear. This can be exasperating, but it can also serve as a reminder of what *not* to do when you write. Even if the information and instructions from a prospective funder are less than clear, we urge you to follow the guidelines for readability we have laid out in this book in your proposals and in all of your communications with funders. Doing this effectively can be a nuanced exercise. It's best to avoid jargon and acronyms specific to your organization or profession. At the same time, if the application uses terms such as "partnering with local agencies" or "entrepreneurial activities" you would want to include that language to demonstrate your understanding of what the funder is looking for.

When you write a grant proposal, you are usually competing with many others for a limited amount of money. Real people read and evaluate every proposal. You must convince them that what you are proposing is sound and will give them the biggest bang for their buck. This means attending to the basics of spelling, punctuation, and grammar. While this may seem obvious, it can be hard to remember to proofread when you are writing under the pressure of a deadline. Writing errors suggest a lack of attention to detail, which in turn may call into question your ability to successfully carry out the project for which you are requesting funding.

Using active voice in a funding proposal leaves no question about who will do what. Make it as easy as you can for reviewers to evaluate the merits of your proposal. As one grant-writing expert puts it:

Clarity is everything. . . . For grants, the best style is straightforward and simple. Avoid unnecessary jargon, long paragraphs, long sentences, and unfamiliar words. Consciously or unconsciously, many grant writers try to impress their readers with unfamiliar phrases, high-toned language, and complex writing. This is all wrong: By far, the best proposals are also the clearest. (Henson, 2003, n.p.).

Example 6.4 illustrates the difference between a grant writer who is trying to impress and one who is using straightforward, simple language.

Example 6.4	**Trying to Impress versus Straightforward and Simple**
Trying to Impress	Straightforward and Simple
A family-oriented drop-out prevention educational program will be developed and disseminated by the knowledgeable and well-trained staff hired to implement this project. This multi-faceted educational program will be disseminated to families meeting eligibility criteria as determined by the program's required eligibility screening protocol. Compliance with project timelines will be ensured with certitude by adherence to a systematic review of written reports submitted by project staff on a weekly basis. This system of identifying barriers and challenges will facilitate the delivery of results in order to ensure timely outcomes.	Our agency will develop a drop-out prevention educational program for families. Families will fill out an application to determine their eligibility to participate in the program. To ensure that the project is completed on time, staff will file weekly progress reports. These reports will enable project leaders to identify and promptly respond to any barriers or challenges that arise.

We know, from comments we have received on our own grant applications, that reviewers appreciate being able to understand exactly what we are proposing. A clearly written, easily understood application helps your proposal stand out and assures the funders that they know exactly what you are asking them to fund. After all, if you can't explain clearly what you propose to do with their money, how can they have confidence that you will be able to plan and carry out your proposed project? Although we have neither the space nor the expertise to explore the topic of grant writing in detail, you may wish to visit the Foundation Center's Grant Space website (www.grantspace.org) where you will find more detailed information on developing proposals, a variety of sample grant documents, and other resources for human service organizations.

APPEALING TO DONORS AND VOLUNTEERS

Donors

As with board members, donors, potential donors, and volunteers are typically a diverse group of people. These audiences include individuals who already know about your work and want to help your agency as well as those who will help if you can convince them of the importance of doing so. Most donors and potential donors are not likely to be experts on the programs and services you provide or the clients you serve. As is true for other audiences, they need a context for your request.

Think about what matters to a donor. First and foremost, donors want to know that the money they give you will be used for programs and services that mean something to them. Any request for donations should clearly state whom you help, how you help, and what a donation will support. Whether your agency offers services directly to individuals, families, and groups or provides education and outreach to an entire community, state, or region, many donors want to know how your agency makes a difference. If there are measurable outcomes from your programs and services, cite them. This demonstrates that donations can make a difference. Keeping your focus on what donors need to know and explaining these topics in plain language will help motivate them and keep them interested in your agency and its work.

Example 6.5 is an example of a poorly written donor letter. Beginning the letter with statistics before the reader has any idea why the letter cites those statistics may result in readers responding with "so what?" Example 6.6 is a revised version of the letter that attempts to grab readers' attention in the first sentence and tells them what they need to know.

Example 6.5   Letter to Donors

Dear Safe Place Supporter:

Approximately 7,000 adolescents are reported as runaways in our state every year. These runaways are known to be 50 percent more likely to drop out of school and 65 percent more likely to use illegal drugs such as marijuana and even heroin. They have a 70 percent likelihood of becoming involved with the courts. The reasons these adolescents run away are many. Some are fleeing from trouble at home, while others have been influenced by unsavory peers, and still others are having problems at school. No matter what the reason is, these young people need a place to get help. Help us help them by supporting the Safe Place, a shelter for runaways.

Example 6.6   Revised Letter to Donors

Dear Safe Place Supporter:

The Safe Place is a place of safety for young runaways who are often lonely, scared, and desperate. We provide shelter, someone to talk to, and access to health and educational services. We also help families to get back together. The Safe Place offers hope to young people struggling to find their way. Your donation of $20 per month will ensure a brighter future for one of these kids.

Volunteers

If your agency uses volunteers, you know that their contributions can be as important as support from donors. Some types of organizations, such as hospice, Meals on Wheels, and guardian ad litem programs, could not function without volunteers. Volunteers are like other audiences we have discussed; they are interested in what is relevant to them. That usually includes information about volunteer opportunities, specific time requirements, schedules, and the tasks they will be performing.

Volunteers are giving their time. One way to respect their time is to be sure that they can quickly read and understand all of your written communications with them. Use plain language to tell them what they need to know, whether you are conveying your messages through email, an agency website, printed brochures, newsletters, or written instructions for completing volunteer tasks. Volunteers connect your agency to the community by informing community members about your agency's services, programs, and needs. When you provide them with a clear understanding of what your agency does, they can pass along clear and accurate information to others.

COMMUNICATING WITH STAFF

Clear communication is vital within your agency. If you have ever worked in a setting where internal communications were vague, confusing, or contradictory, you know how frustrating that can be.

Staff Recruitment

The first written communication prospective employees usually see is a position advertisement or job description. Those items provide information about the job and the organization. It is to the agency's benefit, as well as that of potential job applicants, for such information to be clearly written. Example 6.7 contains two less-than-clear help-wanted ads that we saw recently. We offer them as a reminder not to assume that job seekers, no matter how well qualified, will be familiar with the language you use inside your agency.

| **Example 6.7** | **Help Wanted Ads** |

Ad #1

Family Resources is a CABHA with both Adult and Child continuum. We are experiencing significant growth and are in need of the following positions. Provisionally Licensed Therapist. Fully Licensed Therapists. Intensive in Home Leads. Intensive in Home Q's. Community support Team Leads. Community Support Team Q's and AP's. DT therapists. Q's and AP's as well as NP's and Psychiatrists. Please send resume to . . .

Ad #2

Trainer to work with a team to adapt Strengths-Based Case Management Model for use in CBS programming for youth with SED ages 15–22. Required qualifications include: Bachelor's Degree in social service or related field or an established expertise in an administrative/supervisory role within the mental health services delivery system. Contact us for a full position description. Equal Opportunity Employer M/F/D/V.

We wouldn't be surprised if reading these ads raised some of the same questions for you as it did for us. What are "intensive in home Q's"? What are "Community Support Team Q's and AP's"? Although we are professionals with experience in health, mental health, and a variety of human service settings, we could not decipher the first ad sufficiently to identify all of the positions for which the agency was recruiting. As for the second ad, not only were we mystified by CBS and SED, it took some searching to discover that the M/F/D/V at the end was an abbreviation for "male/female/disabled/veteran."

In the past, when the only means of advertising open positions was in newspapers, agencies tried to use as little expensive classified ad space as possible. This spawned a vocabulary of abbreviations and acronyms that are often indecipherable. It is true that motivated prospective applicants could look up the unfamiliar acronyms, abbreviations, and jargon in examples 6.7 just as we did (although we suspect they would be no more successful than we were at finding all of them). We would argue that a clearly written ad or job description that most people can understand is the best way to recruit new employees.

The Internet has significantly changed the nature of employee recruitment. Now most human service agencies post positions online rather than printing them in a newspaper. There is no longer a need to save space, and therefore money, by using the abbreviations and acronyms that filled the want ads for decades. Websites listing jobs provide much more room to be specific about the job for which you are recruiting. Nonetheless, we urge you to be both clear *and* concise when you write a job ad or position description. One way to be sure your ad is clear is to have someone who is not familiar with your agency or the position read it before you post it. Ask the person to point out anything that doesn't make sense. This will provide you with feedback on how readable your ad is and enable you to clarify anything that might be unclear or confusing.

In example 6.8, we suggest a revision to simplify and clarify the first ad in example 6.7. In the second ad, we would classify "strengths-based case management" as jargon. If the agency is looking for someone who has specific training in something specifically called the Strengths-Based Case Management Model, the ad should say that. If not, it would be better to leave it out and simply explain the skills or tasks involved. As for the acronyms, they should be spelled out because we doubt we're the only ones who could not decipher them.

Example 6.8 **Help Wanted Ad Revised**

Family Resources is a growing nonprofit mental health agency serving children, adults, and families. We are hiring for a number of positions, including psychiatrists, nurses, therapists, and community support workers. Please visit our website at www.familyresources.org for more information about the open positions and to submit your resume.

We used these examples to point out that the first communication a human service agency has with employees is before it hires them. Possibly, the agencies that wrote the ads wanted to screen out anyone who didn't speak their agency language. If that was not their objective, the acronyms, abbreviations, and jargon might have caused these agencies to miss out on qualified applicants who did not understand what positions the agencies were trying to fill or the qualifications required for those positions. Another concern we would have is that if an agency cannot clearly specify what it is looking for when recruiting staff, perhaps other aspects of agency communication also lack clarity.

Internal Communications

Internal communications are vital to the effective functioning of any agency. These communications may be face to face, electronic, or print based. Our interest, of course, is in those that take place through the written word, whether it is transmitted electronically or printed on paper. There is no guarantee that every recipient will read any message in its entirety. However, if an agency's internal communications are often unclear, wordy, or filled with irrelevant details, employees may not open or read them at all. Ambiguous messages from the executive staff can result in assumptions, rumors, and suspicions that negatively affect staff morale and overall agency functioning. And if requests for action do not clearly state who is supposed to do what and when they are to do it, the outcome may be confusion and inaction.

In many human service agencies, policies and procedures are another facet of internal communication that can benefit from improved readability. Policies and procedures that are written in obscure, bureaucratic language are of little practical value if no one can understand what they mean or how to apply them. Writing policies and procedures can be a tedious and thankless job. However, separating the need-to-know content from the nice-to-know, replacing unnecessarily big words with plain language, and shortening long, complex sentences can help bring clarity to these vital communications. For those who do turn to policies and procedures for guidance, there is nothing more frustrating than finding that, after reading it, you know no more about how to proceed than you did before you read it. As illustrated in example 6.9, even the most mundane policy can be needlessly complicated. We think people would be much more likely to read and understand the three-sentence rewrite.

Example 6.9	**Rewriting a Complicated Policy**
Original Policy	Rewritten Policy
The control of traffic and parking is required to protect the safety of everyone and to permit the conduct of the organization's business. Lack of space is not a valid excuse for violating parking regulations. The regulations stipulate where parking is authorized rather than where it is improper to park. The fact that a person parks in violation of any regulation or law and does not receive a citation does not mean that no violation has occurred. Responsibility for finding a legal parking space rests with the motor vehicle operator.	Everyone must obey parking regulations. You may park only where parking is allowed. Anyone who parks illegally risks getting a citation.

Email

In chapter 7 we will discuss the opportunities and pitfalls in digital communications such as websites, texting, and social media. Here we want to focus briefly on email. If you write clear, concise emails, you increase the likelihood that recipients will read your messages, understand them, and accurately interpret the tone you intend to convey.

Tone communicates your attitude or feelings about the subject or the person to whom you are sending the message. When we talk to people face to face, others can see our body language and facial expressions, which convey our attitudes and feelings. When we talk on the telephone, we provide cues about our attitudes and feelings through changes in tone of voice and speech patterns. When we communicate by email, none of these signals are available to provide a context for the words. "Because contextualization cues indicate how an utterance should be interpreted, their absence [in email] increases the likelihood of misunderstandings, especially in terms of conversational tone or tenor" (Gordon & Luke, 2012, p. 120).

Email enables us to respond quickly. Sometimes we may respond so quickly that we fail to notice that the words we write convey a tone that is less than positive. If the message is about any topic that has the potential to be misunderstood, or if you are upset with the recipient, set the message aside for a short time and reread it before you click "send." If you suspect your tone might come across as negative, read it out loud or, even better, ask a colleague to read the message and give you comments on the tone and suggestions for making it more positive.

A positive tone should come across as respectful, friendly, and professional. Being respectful begins with determining whether to use first names or formal titles such as Ms., Mr., or Dr. Using a first name, unless you are sure the other person prefers it, may come across as overly friendly and unprofessional. Look at how your correspondents sign their messages to you. If they sign off with their first name, it is probably acceptable to address them that way in return. Otherwise, we suggest erring on the side of formality. Be careful too, about using exclamation points to indicate a positive tone. Using a lot of exclamation points—and some would say using any exclamation points at all—is not professional. As for emoticons such as smiley faces, they do not belong in professional correspondence.

Figure 6.1	Quick Tips for Writing Clear, Readable, Professional Email

- Always fill in the subject line with a topic that means something to your reader. For example, not "Food Bank" or "Important!" but "Food Bank Supplies Are Getting Low."
- Put your main point in the opening sentence.
- Do not use ALL CAPITALS. This is the electronic equivalent of shouting.
- Do not use all lower-case letters. This is the electronic equivalent of mumbling.

- Use proper grammar and punctuation and avoid textspeak (the shorthand used in texting). You may be ROFLOL (rolling on floor laughing out loud), but your reader may be left wondering WUWT (what's up with that).

- Be brief and polite. If your message runs longer than two or three short paragraphs, consider (a) reducing the message or (b) providing an attachment.

- Add a signature block with appropriate contact information (in most cases, your name, business address, and phone number, along with any legal disclaimer required by your organization). Do you need to clutter the signature block with a clever quotation and artwork? Probably not.

- Edit and proofread before hitting "send."

- Reply promptly to serious messages. If you need more than a day to collect information or make a decision, send a brief response acknowledging you received the email and explaining the delay. (Nordquist, 2013)

Figure 6.1 lists other tips for improving email messages. No matter who your audience is for an email, this principle still holds: tell them what they *need* to know. If you have a small nugget of information, just say it. Do not be guilty of sending a long, convoluted message like the one in example 6.10. We have no idea why the person who wrote this message did not simply say: "Please note that our office's 555-1213 line has been disconnected. Our main number is still 555-1212."

Example 6.10   A Convoluted Email

Greetings all:

We have changed telephone systems. Our main office number is the same as it always has been, 555-1212. That being said, before we changed systems, we also had 555-1213 as our second "roll-over" line. With the new system we no longer need the roll-over line; the new system can stack calls on a single line. The 555-1213 line has been disconnected. I have noticed that some of you did use the 555-1213 line to contact the main office. If you are in the habit of using this number, please note you will now need to use 555-1212.

COMMUNICATING WITH THE MEDIA

Many books have been written on how to communicate effectively with the media. Because our emphasis in this book is on creating readable written materials, we will focus here on press releases. Press releases can be an effective way to spread the word about your agency's events and accomplishments. As with other professional writing, sticking to the guidelines for readability increases the chances your press release will be published and that, if it is published, people will read and understand it.

For press releases, journalists want the facts, not hype. We actually knew one journalist who always used a black marker to cross out every adjective and exclamation point in a press release before he read it. While this may seem extreme, it's a good reminder that what the media is looking for is need-to-know information without any unnecessary details.

Some of our tips for press releases will sound pretty familiar by now. Use short words, short sentences, and avoid jargon and acronyms. Check your grammar and punctuation for errors. Write in the active voice; stay focused on the facts, and make sure your message clearly provides need-to-know information. There is one significant difference between writing for the audiences we have discussed so far and writing a press release. In a press release, do not use the first person. Instead of "we" or "our," use the third person: the agency, the spokesperson, the staff. No matter how excited you are about the subject of the press release, never use exclamation points. Finally, improve your chances that the media will pay attention to your press releases by presenting your news in the standard format illustrated in example 6.11.

Example 6.11	Press Release Format

FOR IMMEDIATE RELEASE

CONTACT: Contact person's name and title, organization name, phone number, email address

Headline: A brief, clear statement of the key point.

Date, city, and state

First paragraph: Two sentences that provide a quick overview of the news or event and why it is important. Include who, what, when, and where.

Second paragraph: Provide some background information on the program or event. Explain what makes the news or event important.

Last paragraph: Briefly describe your organization. Include a summary of other events or happenings and a brief agency history. The last sentence should be: "For more information, contact . . ."

###

(Center the symbol ### under the last sentence to indicate the end of the press release.)

REFERENCES

Caroselli, M. (2000). *Leadership skills for managers*. New York, NY: McGraw-Hill.

Gordon, C., & Luke, M. (2012). Discursive negotiation of face via email: Professional identity development in school counseling supervision. *Linguistics and Education, 23*, 112–122. doi: http://dx.doi.org/10.1016/j.linged.2011.05.002.

Henson, K. T. (2003). Debunking some myths about grant writing. *Chronicle of Higher Education*, June 26. Retrieved from http://chronicle.com/article/Debunking-Some-Myths-About/45256.

Masaoka, J. (2010). *Five tips for better board packets*. Board Café, October 4. Retrieved from http://www.blueavocado.org/node/581.

Nordquist, R. (2013). Ten tips on how to write a professional email. Retrieved from http://grammar.about.com/od/developingessays/a/profemails.htm.

Readability and Electronic Communication

If you look at the various strategies available for dealing with a new technology, sticking your head in the sand is not the most plausible strategy.

—Ralph C. Merkle

Print is the primary medium nonprofits and social service agencies use to communicate with their clients, and it is not likely to disappear. However, since the early 1990s, the use and availability of electronic/digital information has increased dramatically. (Note: we have used the terms *electronic* and *digital* interchangeably to discuss information that is transmitted electronically.) Advances in digital technology can open up new avenues for communication, service delivery, and community organization. In this chapter we address current popular electronic media, including Facebook, Twitter, websites, text messaging, and mobile technologies. Although we know that technology changes rapidly and will continue to evolve, we hope the information here will provide a foundation for any writing you do for digital media.

Advances in electronic communications have the potential to change the way human service agencies interact with and communicate to various stakeholders, including clients, donors, volunteers, and the community at large. Electronic communications include websites, email, text messages, and social media. The term *social media* refers to "forms of electronic communication . . . through which users create online communities to share information, ideas, personal messages, and other content" (*Merriam-Webster's Online Dictionary*). Popular forms of social media include Facebook, Twitter, and Pinterest.

If your agency is to use electronic communications effectively, it is important to know who uses them and how they go about it. It's equally important to find out what barriers may limit your target population's access to and use of digital communications. Just as you do not want to offer print materials your audience cannot comprehend, it is critical that any forms of electronic communication you use with clients are accessible, readable, and user-friendly. You want to be sure that you don't deliver important information electronically that your audience cannot understand or use.

Although this chapter deals with electronic communication, we wish to emphasize that integrating electronic media into your overall communications with clients and others does not eliminate the need for printed material. Do not make critical information available only in a digital format. Some people have no access to electronic communication. Others may want or need a piece of paper instead of or in addition to what is available electronically.

THE DIGITAL DIVIDE

More people have access to the Internet than ever before (Zikuhr & Smith, 2012). Despite increasingly widespread access, there is a digital divide that separates people who live in high-poverty areas, older adults, and individuals with less education than a high school diploma from those who take access for granted (Napoli & Obar, 2013). It's true that public libraries and many community centers provide Internet access to low-income communities (Bertot, McClure, & Jaeger, 2008; Powell, Bryne, & Dailey, 2010), but in many public facilities, the demand is so great that people's time online is limited. The rising use of mobile devices, including smartphones, has increased the ability of previously underserved people to use the Internet. Although 87 percent of adults who use the Internet do so with a mobile device (Pew Research Center, 2014), Sorenson and colleagues (2014) found that 99 percent of 261 domestic violence agency homepages made no mention of a mobile version. This suggests that either agencies are not creating versions for mobile devices, or they are not informing website users of their existence.

It's important to be aware, however, that there is more to access than possessing a smartphone. Smartphones do not provide the same quality or quantity of information as computers. So while it may seem to make sense to provide an online application form for your agency's services, if much of your target audience has no computer and connects to the Internet with a smartphone, it will be difficult—if not impossible—for them to complete and submit that application electronically. To fully take advantage of the Internet requires high-speed connections that are available only to those who can afford expensive cable service contracts.

Although mobile devices are narrowing some aspects of the digital divide, one in five American adults does not use the Internet at all, regardless of access. Those least likely to use the Internet include adults age 65 and older, adults without a high school education, individuals with yearly household incomes below $30,000, and people with disabilities (Zikuhr & Smith, 2012). If your agency serves clients from these groups, you will want to be especially cautious about the kind of information you make available primarily through electronic means. Even if your clients have smartphones, research indicates that individuals whose access to the Internet is through mobile devices rather than computers are less likely to seek information online (Napoli & Obar, 2013).

You can see from table 7.1 that all demographic groups show a dramatic increase in Internet usage from 2000 to 2011. In fact, the only groups with lower than 50 percent usage are seniors over age 65 and individuals without a high school diploma. For these populations, the main barrier to using the Internet may not be access. It could be the belief that the Internet is not relevant to them, or they may lack the computer skills needed to effectively use it. This means it is important for you to understand as much as you can about your agency's target audience and how they use the Internet and social media, if at all, so that you are communicating with them in a way that is effective. This knowledge is what should drive how much you rely on electronic media. However, even if your client base is unlikely to use it, electronic media may help you reach volunteers, donors, and the general public. It can be a key component of expanding your agency's visibility and outreach to the community.

The information in table 7.1 can serve as a useful guide for developing or updating an agency media strategy. For example, younger people are much more comfortable with social media and texting. If your agency serves adolescents or young adults, developing a strategic plan to incorporate these

Table 7.1	Demographics of Internet Users in 2000 and 2011		
		Percent of adults who use the Internet	
		June 2000	August 2011
	All adults (age 18+)	**47%**	**78%**
	Men	50	80
	Women	45	76
	Race/ethnicity		
	White, non-Hispanic	49	80
	Black, non-Hispanic	35	71
	Hispanic*	40	68
	Age		
	18–29	61	94
	30–49	57	87
	50–64	41	74
	65+	12	41
	Household income		
	Less than $30,000/yr	28	62
	$30,000–$49,999	50	83
	$50,000–$74,999	67	90
	$75,000+	79	97
	Educational attainment		
	No high school diploma	16	43
	High school graduate	33	71
	Some college	62	88
	College and above	76	94

*Note: The 2000 survey included only English-speaking Hispanics. The 2011 survey included both English- and Spanish-speaking Hispanics. All differences are statistically significant except for those between blacks and Hispanics in 2011.

Sources: The Pew Research Center, Internet American Life Project, May 2000 Tracking Survey, conducted May 19 to June 21, 2000; N = 2,117 adults age 18 and older; interviews were conducted in English. The Pew Research Center, Internet and American Life Project, August 2011 Tracking Survey, conducted July 25 to August 26, 2011; N = 2,260 adults age 18 and older; interviews were conducted in both English and Spanish, including 916 interviews conducted by cell phone. More information can be found at pewinternet.org/Static-Pages/Trend-Data/Whos-Online.aspx.

digital formats into your overall communications would make sense (Duggan & Brenner, 2013). If, on the other hand, you work primarily with low-income seniors, relying on text messaging or a Twitter feed is unlikely to be an effective way to reach them.

THE DIGITAL ADVANTAGE

Digital communications do have some advantages over print, including the immediacy of the information, ease of updating, and interactivity. Print materials can quickly go out of date, thus providing inaccurate or unhelpful information. Constantly updating and reprinting paper-based communications is expensive and time-consuming, and unfortunately, too often it does not happen as often as it should. Updating a website or changing an online form is usually fast and inexpensive once you have the website infrastructure in place. However, just as agencies should update print materials regularly, they must also keep websites, Facebook pages, and other online communications current and fresh. This requires having a designated staff person or someone on contract to maintain and update the website, refresh status updates on social media, and monitor and respond to the interactive features of these technologies.

It's important to remember that websites can become just as out of date as print materials. Facebook pages that haven't had a status update in three months don't encourage people to check in very often, and that defeats the purpose of the page to begin with. It may be fast and easy to update a Facebook page or add a new service to your website, but this doesn't happen by magic. Unless someone is explicitly assigned to manage these communication tools, they may harm rather than help your agency's image.

The interactivity of digital communication is another potential advantage, one that research indicates most nonprofits, including human service agencies, are not exploiting (Jaskyte, 2012; Waters, Burnett, Lamm, & Lucas, 2009). It allows you to tailor information to the needs and interests of clients as well as others affiliated in some way with your agency. For example, if you plan a program for clients or a training session for volunteers, you can post an announcement or invitation with the details on a Facebook page and/or text it to prospective attendees and ask them to respond if they plan to participate.

If you have, or plan to develop, a Facebook page for your agency, suggestions for maximizing its potential include using it to:

- link back to your agency website;
- distribute organizational news;
- publicize educational and fundraising campaigns;
- post press releases; and
- provide a list of volunteer opportunities. (Waters et al., 2009)

One key distinction between digital and print communications is that the recipients of your digital messages can spread those messages themselves by sharing them on Facebook or re-tweeting them on Twitter. For example, if you use Twitter, you can tweet a message about food bank shortages and have your Twitter followers re-tweet your message to help you get the word out quickly. Therefore, it is important to make sure your messages are relevant, clear, and are valuable enough to the recipients to motivate them to pass them on.

CREATING A READABLE WEBSITE

The goal of a human service agency website should be to empower clients by giving them "credible information about agency services, eligibility, fees, location, and staff qualifications" (Vernon & Lynch, 2003, p. 38). There is no advantage to developing and maintaining an agency website if the content is not clearly written or if the website layout is confusing, distractingly busy, or difficult to navigate. Sadly, the research to date indicates that human service organizations are not doing a very good job of creating user-friendly, easy-to-read websites for people with limited literacy skills and people with disabilities (Fitzsimmons, Michael, Hulley, & Scott, 2010; Friedmeyer-Trainor, Vernon, & Lynch, 2012; Sorenson, Shi, Zhang, & Xue, 2014).

Applying the guidelines for readability to your agency's electronic communications will help make your website a useful tool for communicating with anyone who arrives there. There are some specific issues that are relevant if you expect clients with limited literacy skills to find and use your website. First of all, they may have problems spelling the terms they are searching for, and they may have trouble sorting through search results to find what they need. They may also have difficulty distinguishing advertisements from noncommercial informational or educational websites (Birru et al., 2004). People with limited literacy skills face challenges in navigating the Internet that may be so overwhelming to them that they give up without finding what they are looking for.

To make your agency website helpful to clients with limited literacy skills, as well as to anyone else who uses it, you need to understand some basics about how search engines work, what makes a website interface user-friendly, and how to organize the information you are presenting. As a human services professional, this may initially strike you as being well beyond your comfort zone. Rest assured that you do not need to be a techie or a computer programmer to create a smart, useful website that people can easily find when they search.

If you are assigned to create or assist in the creation of an agency website, some very basic technical knowledge will help you ask the right questions and know what to look for when working with a technology professional. If you understand the basics of how to make a website appear at the top of relevant search results, and what makes a website easy to use, your agency can create a useful, readable online presence.

How Search Engines Work

When you conduct a search using Google or another search engine, the search engine sends out "spiders." A spider is a program that follows links throughout the Internet, analyzes keywords in websites and online documents, and uses them to find matches for your search. Keywords are words that stand out as relevant to the content of a website or document. They do not have to be single words. In fact, most keywords are comprised of two or more words. For example, if someone is searching for "gang prevention programs," most search engines are sophisticated enough to recognize "gang prevention" as a concept and may return results that include any of the keywords on the sample list in example 7.1. Understanding these basics about search engines is important because when you write the text for your website you should be sure to include keywords that people may search for. To maximize the effectiveness of your keywords, you should be sure they appear in the titles and subtitles on your website, because search engine spiders put more weight on keywords in prominent locations.

Example 7.1	Sample Keyword List for a Gang Prevention Program

- Gang prevention
- Afterschool programs
- Gang intervention
- Gang alternatives
- Youth crime
- At-risk youth
- Gangs
- Bloods
- Crips
- Keeping kids out of gangs
- Positive youth development
- Mentoring at-risk youth
- Gang mediation
- Why kids join gangs

To develop your list of keywords, it's a good idea to brainstorm the search terms people might use to look for your agency's programs and services. We suggest you consult with agency colleagues but also, if possible, ask clients what words they might look for if they were seeking the kind of assistance your agency provides. In other words, try to think from the potential user's perspective, rather than only from the perspective of agency insiders. One easy way to find out how clients would search is to have staff members ask them, during routine contacts, what words they would use to look for the services you offer. For example, while you may think of your facility as an "emergency crisis shelter," a runaway teen who needs a place to stay is probably going to search for a "runaway shelter."

While all of this focus on keywords makes sense because of their role in attracting search engine spiders, preparing text with an eye on keywords can complicate the writing process. Writing for readability may seem incompatible with writing for search engines because you will want to incorporate keywords as much as possible without compromising the readability of your copy. This can be a delicate balance. In order to make the process easier and less complex, it helps to develop a list of the keywords you will want to include in your website copy before you start writing.

If your agency's budget allows, you can hire an expert on search engine optimization (commonly abbreviated as SEO). Simply put, search engine optimization means doing what is necessary to ensure that your website comes up at the top of the search engine results. Search engine optimization experts can be found in any media agency that creates websites for clients. There are also independent contractors who can help with your search engine optimization efforts. If you ask, you may find that your agency has board members or volunteers with this expertise, or these individuals may be able to recommend an expert to assist with this. Before you hire an expert, however, you may wish to review the practical information and cautions on search engine optimization that Google offers (http://support.google.com/webmasters/bin/answer.py?hl=en&answer=35291).

In addition to finding keywords that are in prominent locations on your website, search engine spiders also look for meta tags. Meta tags are hidden from people visiting your site, but they are seen by the search engines. The most important thing to know about meta tags is that they include keywords and a description of the page's content. Well-written meta tags will help your website come up at or near the top when people are searching for what you offer. You can have as many meta tags as you need to boost your placement in search results.

It's a good idea, especially if you work with low-literacy populations, to include misspellings of search terms in your meta tags. This is also helpful for older adults because they are more likely than younger people to make typographical errors (Nielsen, 2005). For example, if you provide housing assistance, you might want to include "hsouing assistance" and "housing assistence" in your meta tags. While it would be impossible to include all potential misspellings, anticipating some of the more common misspellings or typographical errors can be immensely helpful. Anyone who has the skills to help you create a website should be knowledgeable about meta tags, keyword placement, and other ways to make it easier for people to find your website.

Making Your Website Easy to Use

Once people in your community, including clients, can find you on the Internet, it's time to make sure your website is easy for them to use. If you want to create a user-friendly website, it's helpful to understand how people read web content. Research indicates that most individuals scan the page, and very few actually read it word by word (Weinreich, Obendorf, Herder, & Mayer, 2008; Whitenton, 2014). Research has found that individuals with limited literacy skills do not have the ability to scan text for information (Nielson, 2005). Just as they do when reading print materials, they read digital text word for word. If they see blocks of densely written text, long words, and long sentences, they will not attempt to read it. Nielsen (2005) suggests the following for making websites readable for people with limited literacy skills:

1. Limit your homepage to the sixth grade reading level. Keep other pages no higher than eighth grade level.
2. Put the most important information at the top of the page. Poor readers do not scroll down to look for information.
3. Do not use text that moves or changes. Poor readers can most easily read text that stands still. People with impaired motor skills also have difficulty following moving text or images.
4. Keep the text in a single column so readers don't have to scan the page to find the information they're looking for. This makes the text easier to view on a smartphone. It also helps those with vision impairments and people whose first language is not English.
5. Use a linear menu for the main content. A linear menu takes users from one page to the next in the same way an online tutorial does. This helps them understand the next place to go without having to scan the page for options.

Nielsen (1997) and Sorenson and colleagues (2014) suggest a number of elements you can incorporate to make the text on your website easier for people to read. You may notice some parallels between these recommendations and the guidelines for readability we emphasize throughout this book:

1. Use bulleted lists instead of paragraphs whenever possible.
2. Use meaningful subheads that draw the reader to a block of information.
3. Use one idea per paragraph.
4. Use half the word count of conventional writing.
5. Use short words and short sentences.

Additionally, many of the same layout and design guidelines we provided in chapter 3 that make print easy to read also apply to the layout and design of web pages:

1. Do not use all caps.
2. Use ragged right margins instead of justified (i.e., even) right margins.
3. Emphasize important points by underlining, using boldface, or surrounding them with white space.
4. Do not use fancy fonts or a variety of different fonts.
5. Use serif fonts for blocks of copy.
6. Do not use very small fonts.
7. Do not use center alignment for blocks of text.
8. Leave plenty of white space.
9. Use images related to the text to help convey the meaning of the words.

Another element that will make your website more user-friendly, especially for low-literacy visitors, is to include your agency's phone number, address, email address, and hours of operation prominently on the homepage. Some individuals may prefer or find it easier to speak with someone in person or on the phone rather than trying to find information on your website. If they have questions, offering contact information gives them a means to ask their questions directly.

If yours is a large agency with many programs and services, you do not need to provide details about every program on your homepage. Instead, provide links to each program. Organize information in ways that will make sense to the people you want to reach. For example, if you offer services for families, you can direct users to links for "Services for Children" and "Services for Parents" which people can follow to find the specific information they are looking for.

Organizing Your Content for Effective Communication

Organizing your content in a thoughtful and logical manner will help to make your website easy to read, especially for clients with limited literacy skills. One of the best ways to organize your information is to make a flow chart before you actually design your website. The purpose of the flow chart is to illustrate how users can easily get to the information they need. Your primary goal should be for users to be able to find the information they need with as few clicks as possible. Think about websites you may have visited that were frustrating and time-consuming because you had to click around to find what you were looking for. Keeping the navigation simple and straightforward will make your website user-friendly.

The sample flowchart in figure 7.1 is very simple. For your agency website, there may be times when you will want to provide access to an additional level of detail or link to an online form. However, if your flowchart becomes very complex, you may need to rethink how easy it will be

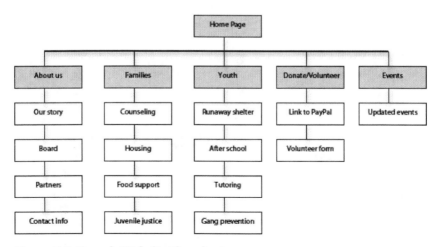

Figure 7.1 Sample Website Flowchart

for people to use your website. Keep in mind that the website flowchart is an internal document and does not necessarily contain the exact wording you will use on the website itself. The idea is to develop a way to organize your website content so it makes sense to people who visit your site.

When you are developing your flowchart, think about the various audiences you are trying to reach and what is likely to be most important to them. The flowchart in figure 7.1 is organized around three basic audiences: the youth that the agency serves, the families of some of the youths served, and the donors and volunteers who support the agency. Each of these audiences is probably looking for different information. By organizing the website in this manner, visitors to the site can quickly get to the information that is relevant to them with just a few clicks.

If you are setting out to develop a website for your agency, you do not need to reinvent the wheel. You can learn a lot by looking at the websites of agencies that serve similar clienteles, and you can assess how easy they are to use. Is the homepage structured in a logical way that guides you directly to what you are looking for? Is it so complex that it is difficult to find the information you're seeking? If you can find a website that is inviting, informative, and easy to navigate, use it as a model for building your own. One helpful idea that we suggest human service agencies incorporate is a "How to Use This Website" page that explains in plain language how to use website features and what users can expect to find.

Another design consideration is making sure your website is readable on a smartphone or other handheld device. As discussed earlier in this chapter, if your website is not accessible via a mobile device, you may not reach the people you hope to reach. There are two options for creating mobile-friendly websites. A *responsive web design* automatically displays content tailored to the user's device. It's fast and efficient but is also expensive to develop. For agencies with limited budgets, it's less costly to use *adaptive web design*, which takes users to a specific page designed for the type of device they are using (Creedon, 2014). The person or agency responsible for building your website should be able to help you incorporate mobile-friendly design into your website.

When you are thinking about how to make your website more mobile-friendly, less is more. Given the small size of the screen on a typical smartphone, most people will have difficulty reading a lot of dense copy to find what they need. Keep it short and to the point and use bulleted lists and links as much as possible. One benefit of writing this way is that it encourages you to separate need-to-know information from the nice-to-know content by focusing on what is most important to your audience. Remember to put yourself in your readers' shoes. Keep in mind what they really care about or what they are likely to be looking for. This will improve the usability and readability of your site on a mobile device.

One final consideration when you are creating a website is to be mindful of its accessibility to people with disabilities. Many people with disabilities use assistive technologies. For example, screen readers for the blind speak the text that users cannot see. Voice recognition software allows people who have difficulty using a mouse or who are visually impaired to use verbal commands. Federally funded agencies are mandated to make all of their digital information comply with the Americans with Disabilities Act (US Department of Justice Civil Rights Division, 2003). These standards include guidelines designed to ensure that people with disabilities are not inadvertently excluded from access to websites and other digital information. We have provided a few of those guidelines in figure 7.2. Although this information is somewhat technical, we have included it so that if you are working with an expert to develop or update an agency website, you will be able to request and discuss these considerations.

Figure 7.2	Website Accessibility Guidelines

1. Incorporate into the coding of all new web pages accessible elements including alt tags (which allow a screen reader to describe a visual image), long descriptions, and captions.

2. Include alt tags and/or long descriptions for any images such as photos, graphics, scanned images, or image maps. These descriptions can be hidden from view on the page but are picked up by the screen readers which then read aloud what is represented in images.

3. Make the elements of any online forms and tables accessible.

4. Provide documents in text, not as a single image, when you post them on the website even if you also provide them in another format such as Portable Document Format (PDF). (US Department of Justice Civil Rights Division, 2003)

Testing Your Website for Readability

Once you have created or updated your website, there are some helpful technological tools that can help you analyze reading grade level. Just as with print materials, reading grade level is one indicator of readability. Keeping the reading grade level at eighth grade or lower and incorporating the layout and design guidelines provided earlier in this chapter will help you achieve maximum readability. There are online tools that allow you to analyze the reading grade level of website content by either typing in the website address or cutting and pasting text. They use standard readability formulas to calculate reading grade level. Here are three of these sites:

The Readability Test Tool (www.read-able.com/)

Juicy Studio (http://juicystudio.com/services/readability.php)

Tests Document Readability On-Line Utility (www.online-utility.org/english/readability_test_and_improve.jsp)

USING SOCIAL MEDIA EFFECTIVELY

Social media can be an inexpensive and effective means of communicating with agency stakeholders and staying connected with your various constituencies. This is especially true if your target audience is mostly made up of people younger than 30 and is predominantly female and urban (Duggan & Brenner, 2013). Through these media you can communicate immediately and directly with clients, donors, volunteers, and the community at large.

It can be a challenge to incorporate readability guidelines into your writing when you're using these fast-paced forms of electronic communication. The keys to keeping your writing clear and easy for people with limited literacy skills to understand include:

- Keep it simple. If you have only 140 characters, as is the case with Twitter, you must use words economically. This means eliminating words that don't add to the point you are trying to make, words such as *however, first of all*, or *finally*. Decide on your point, state it, and stop. (Centers for Disease Control and Prevention, 2012).

■ Avoid using "textspeak." It is common practice to substitute "u" for "you" in social media to save on precious character count. For people with limited literacy skills, this is confusing and defeats the purpose of your communication.

■ Use hyperlinks to provide additional information. Create an eye-catching or interesting hook to grab people's attention, then link to more detailed information.

■ Stick to one idea per post. If your agency has a lot of activity going on, you may be tempted to include too much in a single posting. Keep your communication clear by avoiding this temptation. There is no additional cost, and little additional time, required for multiple tweets or posts.

ADDITIONAL RESOURCES

It is not possible to tell you in a single chapter everything you need to know about electronic/digital communication, nor do we know everything you need to know about this topic. Should you wish to pursue it further, we have listed a few resources you may find helpful.

■ A glossary of social media terms: www.socialbrite.org/sharing-center/glossary/

■ Guidelines for developing an agency social media policy: www.idealware.org/articles/story-social-media-policy

■ Suggestions for using mobile technology for fund-raising: http://philanthropy.com/article/Nonprofits-Race-To-Get-Ahead/137793/

REFERENCES

Bertot, J. C., McClure, C. R., & Jaeger, P. T. (2008). The impacts of free public Internet access on public library patrons and communities. *Library Quarterly, 78*(3), 285–301. doi: http://dx.doi.org/10.1086/588445.

Birru, M. S., Monaco, V. M., Lonelyss, C., Drew, H., Njie, V., Bierria, T., . . . Steinman, R. A. (2004). Internet usage by low-literacy adults seeking health information: An observational analysis. *Journal of Medical Internet*

Research, 6(3), p. e25. doi: http://dx.doi.org/10.2196/jmir.6.3.e25. Retrieved from http://www.jmir.org/2004/3/e25/.

Centers for Disease Control and Prevention. (2012). *CDC's guide to writing for social media.* Retrieved from http://www.cdc.gov/socialmedia/Tools/guidelines/.

Creedon, A. (2014, February). Eleven nonprofits that rock responsive web design. *Nonprofit Quarterly.* Retrieved from https://nonprofitquarterly.org/policysocial-context/23766-11-nonprofits-that-rock-responsive-web-design.html.

Duggan, M., & Brenner, J. (2013). The demographics of social media users—2012 Pew Research Center's Internet and American Life Project. Retrieved from http://www.pewinternet.org/2013/02/14/the-demographics-of-social-media-users-2012/.

Fitzsimmons, P. R., Michael, B. D., Hulley, J. L., & Scott, G. O. (2010). A readability assessment of online Parkinson's disease information. *Journal of the Royal College of Physicians of Edinburgh, 40,* 292–296. doi: 10.4997/JRCPE.2010.401.

Friedmeyer-Trainor, K., Vernon, R., & Lynch, D. (2012). Accessibility and agency website design: Stumbling backwards? A follow-up study. *Journal of Technology in Human Services, 30*(2), 59–71. doi: http://dx.doi.org/10.1080/15228835.2012.700559.

Gehl, J. (2000). Nanotechnology designs for the future—small talk with Ralph C. Merkle. *Ubiquity, 2000* (July). Retrieved from http://dl.acm.org/citation.cfm?id=345496&coll=portal&dl=ACM.

Jaskyte, K. (2012). Exploring potential for information technology innovation in nonprofit organizations. *Journal of Technology in Human Services, 30*(2), 118–127. doi.org/10.1080/15228835.2012.695564.

Lasar, M. (2010). FCC: Open schools to community Internet use. *ARS Technica,* February 19, 2010. Retrieved from: http://arstechnica.com/tech-policy/2010/02/fcc-open-public-schools-to-community-Internet-use/.

Napoli, P. M., & Obar, J. A. (2013 April). Mobile leap-frogging and digital divide policy. New America Foundation. Retrieved from http://mediapolicy.newamerica.net/people/archives/269?type=policydoc.

Nielson, J. (1997). How users read on the Web. Retrieved from http://www.nngroup.com/articles/how-users-read-on-the-web/.

Nielsen, J. (2005). Lower-literacy users: Writing for a broad consumer audience. Retrieved from http://www.nngroup.com/articles/writing-for-lower-literacy-users/.

Pew Research Center. (2014). Pew Research Internet Project: Internet user demographics. Retrieved from http://www.pewinternet.org/data-trend/internet-use/latest-stats/.

Powell, A., Bryne, A., and Dailey, D. (2010). The essential Internet: Digital exclusion in low-income American communities. *Policy & Internet, 2,* 161–192. doi: 10.2202/1944-2866.1058.

Sorenson, S. B., Shi, R., Zhang, J., & Xue, J. (2014). Self-presentation on the Web: Agencies serving abused and assaulted women. *American Journal of Public Health, 104*(4), 702–707.

US Department of Justice Civil Rights Division. (2003). *Accessibility of state and local government websites to people with disabilities.* Retrieved from http://www.ada.gov/websites2.htm.

Vernon, R., & Lynch, D. (2003). Consumer access to agency websites: Our best foot forward? *Journal of Technology in Human Services, 21*(4), 37–51. doi: 10.1300/J017v21n04_03.

Waters, R. D., Burnett, E., Lamm, A., & Lucas, J. (2009). Engaging stakeholders through social networking: How nonprofit organizations are using Facebook. *Public Relations Review, 35*(2), 102–106. doi: http://dx.doi.org/10.1016/j.pubrev.2009.01.006.

Weinreich. H., Obendorf, H., Herder, E., & Mayer, M. (2008). Not quite the average: An empirical study of web use. *ACM Transactions on the Web, 2*(1), 5:2–5:31. doi: 10.1145/1326561.1326566.

Whitenton, K. (2014). Satisficing: Quickly meet users' main needs. Retrieved from http://www.nngroup.com/articles/satisficing/.

Zikuhr, K., & Smith, A. (2012). *Digital differences.* Pew Internet and American Life Project. Retrieved from http://pewInternet.org/Reports/2012/Digital-differences.aspx.

Readability and Documentation

It don't matter weather I can writ good or not—the main thing is that I be able to help my clients.

—Undergraduate social work student quoted in S. J. Wilson,
Recording: Guidelines for Social Workers

When you consider the importance of your documentation, it does matter whether you can "writ good." Poorly written or incomplete documentation has the potential to harm your clients, damage your reputation as a competent professional, put your licensure at risk, and place you and your agency in legal and financial jeopardy. Clearly written records are also a cornerstone of accountable and ethical practice. The codes of ethics of the National Association of Social Workers, the American Association for Marriage and Family Therapy, the American Psychological Association, and the American Counseling Association all mandate that practitioners maintain records of their work with clients (Souders, Strom-Gottfried, & DeVito, 2011). The National Organization for Human Services ethical standards also refer to client records (National Organization for Human Services, n.d.).

The emphasis in this book is on writing readable materials that clients can understand. When you are documenting for your case records, you are writing about, rather than for, clients (although clients do have a legal right to read their case records). We include this chapter on documentation because many of the principles and techniques we have presented for increasing readability will improve your documentation. Good documentation should be so clear that anyone who reads it will know exactly what happened and concise enough so that no one will have to plow through unnecessary details to understand it.

In this chapter, we use the terms *documentation* and *recording* to cover narrative records such as social histories, assessments, progress notes, service plans, and case summaries. We recognize that every agency has its own forms and formats and that the content of your records is determined by your agency's requirements. However, we also believe that no matter where you work there are some basic skills and knowledge that can improve all of your narrative recording.

THE IMPORTANCE OF DOCUMENTATION

The written record provides financial, clinical, and legal accountability, ensures continuity of service, and functions as a tool for supervision and oversight. Let us look briefly at the importance of each of these aspects of documentation:

- Financial accountability: the record verifies to funding sources and third-party payers that your agency is providing the services it is mandated to provide and justifies the funding it receives.
- Clinical accountability: the record demonstrates that you are practicing effectively and ethically and adhering to accepted standards of professional practice.
- Legal accountability: the record can protect you from allegations of malpractice. In a court proceeding, it is the only way to confirm what happened, when and how it happened, what you did and said, and what the client did and said.
- Continuity of service: the record explains the client's situation and what has occurred in the case. This enables others to respond appropriately when you're not available, for example, if a case is transferred to another social worker or if you change jobs.
- Supervision: records provide supervisors with a written account of what has happened with a case. If you are a supervisor, your supervisees' records allow you to keep track of the work they are doing, what they are doing well, and areas where they may need some direction.

■ Oversight: records allow agencies to conduct internal reviews to evaluate the quality and quantity of their services and to assess whether they are meeting critical benchmarks. Internal review results can help agencies identify in-service training needs, plan for current and future needs, and identify strengths and weaknesses in service delivery systems. Internal reviews can enable agencies to correct deficiencies before formal authorities such as licensing and regulatory bodies, governing boards, or third-party payers conduct outside reviews.

WHAT THE RECORD SHOULD INCLUDE

When you are busy with a large caseload, it's easy to put off documentation until the last minute. Keep in mind, however, that one benefit of formal recording is that it gives you a means by which to organize your thinking. Good documentation involves not only writing but also making critical professional judgments about how much or how little to include. Generally, the information that belongs in a case record includes:

1. Relevant demographic data including age, sex, race, and legal status such as court-ordered involuntary commitment

2. A statement of the problem as the client sees it

3. Historical information relevant to proper diagnosis and treatment

4. Assessment procedures such as home visits, interviews, tests, consultations, and evaluations

5. Any formal diagnoses with their factual basis (for example, a psychological diagnosis of clinical depression from a qualified professional or the evidence that supports the diagnosis if you are the qualified professional)

6. Service or treatment plans and goals

7. All agency-related activities that have taken place (interviews, home visits, phone calls, case conferences, court appearances, releases of records). Every entry should include date and place of activities, who was there, what was discussed and observed, the date you wrote the entry, and your signature

8. Written communications with and about clients

9. Ongoing assessments of problems and needs

10. Changes in service or treatment plans or goals

11. A record of any discharge, case transfer or termination and the basis for those actions (Kagel & Kopels, 2008; Sidell, 2011)

Personal Notes

Practitioners sometimes keep personal notes separate from the official record. The intention is often to keep certain information from clients or others who may have access to the record. However, you should be very careful about keeping personal notes in addition to your official records because they can be subpoenaed by the courts (Kagel & Kopels, 2008; Reamer, 2005). Some states have laws that govern human service professionals' use of such notes. If you keep personal notes, you would be wise to find out what your state's laws specify about these notes.

WRITING READABLE DOCUMENTATION

As with other types of professional writing, the foundation for good documentation is correct grammar, punctuation, and spelling. The words you use and the way you use them can either clearly explain or obscure your observations and actions. If your documentation is not well written, anyone inside or outside your agency who reads your progress notes, assessments, case summaries, or reports may form a negative opinion about your competence.

Every agency has its own guidelines for documentation. Although we cannot address your agency's specific documentation requirements or the format your agency uses, there are some generic techniques that are useful for all human service agency documentation. Even though clients are not the audience for your documentation, your supervisor or any other professionals who read your records will appreciate being able to read and immediately understand what you have written. Here are a few general rules for good documentation:

1. Record promptly in your progress notes all interviews and actions taken with and on behalf of clients.

2. Record all entries in chronological order.

3. Begin each entry with the full date of the contact.

4. Refer to yourself consistently in either third person or first person. Many agencies' policies require workers to refer to themselves as "the worker" or "this worker." If your agency does not specify whether to use third or first person, decide which you prefer and use it consistently. Do not use "I" in one sentence and "the worker" in the next. This could be misinterpreted to mean that two different individuals are working with the client.

5. Use agency procedures to document and report any incidents that could result in potential liability.

6. Sign all entries with your full signature (not initials), your title, and the date you wrote the note whether or not it is the same as the date the contact took place.

If you handwrite your notes:

1. Write legibly. Your notes are worthless as a record of your work if you are the only one who can decipher them.

2. Correct an error by drawing a line through it, writing the correction above it, with your initials and the date. If you blot out an error, it could look as though you were trying to hide something.

3. Follow agency procedures about ink color; some agencies require blue ink in order to distinguish originals from copies.

Although the purpose and content of your documentation is quite different from the materials you create for clients, the guidelines for writing clear documentation are similar to those that increase the readability of print materials directed at clients. These seven guidelines apply to all narrative documentation that you include in case records.

1: Use correct grammar, punctuation, and spelling.

Supervisors, colleagues, team members, auditors, judges—anyone who reads your documentation—will form an impression of your competence from what you have written. You are what you write when those who read what you write do not know you. Grammar, punctuation, and spelling errors are distracting and may call into question the accuracy of your documentation.

No matter how skilled you are at working with clients, you are less likely to be taken seriously if your notes contain poor grammar, incorrect punctuation, and misspelled words.

2: Write in active voice.

As we discussed in chapter 2, active voice specifies who did what, and that is exactly why you should use it for your documentation. No one who reads your records should have to guess at or make assumptions about who did what, as they would in example 8.1, where the use of passive voice makes the note quite vague. There is no way to be sure who did what. As example 8.2 illustrates, rewriting the note in active voice leaves no doubt about who did what.

Example 8.1   **Note Written in Passive Voice**

Client's boyfriend's threats were overheard. The police were called when he was seen near client's apartment with a gun. Boyfriend was arrested. Client was taken to the courthouse and a protective order was obtained.

Example 8.2   **Note Written in Active Voice**

Client's neighbor told worker she overheard boyfriend's threats and called police after seeing boyfriend near client's apartment with a gun. Police arrested boyfriend. Worker took client to courthouse where she obtained a protective order.

3: Avoid jargon, acronyms, and abbreviations.

Everyone who works for your agency probably uses and understands the same jargon and acronyms. The agency may also have standard abbreviations that workers use in their documentation. This may work well in-house, but the audience for your records will, at times, include third-party payers, professionals from other agencies, the courts, and clients themselves. Records filled with abbreviations, acronyms, and jargon may be confusing or indecipherable to these audiences. If workers in your agency use a standard set of acronyms, the agency should have a glossary or cheat sheet that defines them, and anytime you share records with an entity outside your agency, the glossary should be included. The same is true for abbreviations, including your own personal abbreviations. Unless your agency has a list of approved abbreviations, do not abbreviate. As you can see in example 8.3, notes that contain personal abbreviations, jargon, and acronyms can be just plain baffling, and it takes time and effort to attempt to decipher them. In case your attempts to do so were not entirely successful, table 8.1 provides some translations.

Example 8.3	Note with Personal Abbreviations, Jargon, and Acronyms

HV w/client and dau. Client discharged from VAMC last week. Worker will assist w/SSI app. Client should qualify based on CHF and associated SOB. Worker finds no need for APS referral at this time. Worker requested psych consult to r/o any MI because of client self-rept of "depression" after bro's suicide. Goals are to empower client and promote self-advocacy and self-efficacy.

Abbreviations		Acronyms		Jargon	
HV	home visit	VAMC	Veterans' Administration Medical Center	empower	develop a sense of control over his life
w/	with	SSI	Supplemental Security Income	self-advocacy	speak up for what he wants and needs
dau	daughter	CHF	congestive heart failure	self-efficacy	believe he can achieve his goals
app	application	SOB	shortness of breath		
psych consult	psychiatric consultation	APS	adult protective services		
r/o	rule out	MI	mental illness		
self-rept	self-report				
bro	brother				

4: Describe the facts.

We advised you to limit the content of materials you write for clients to what your audience *needs* to know. Similarly, when you are documenting for case records, we advise you to limit the content to the facts that are necessary to provide financial, clinical, and legal accountability and to ensure continuity of service. A clear, factual record will enable your supervisor to track your work and provide the agency with the information it needs for internal reviews and audits. What are the facts? For progress notes they include:

- When the contact took place. In addition to the day, month, and year, in some settings you may want—or be required—to record the time as well.
- Where the contact took place. Was it in your office, at the client's home, in a residential care facility, by telephone?
- Who was there. Be sure to note if there were family members, friends, neighbors, team members, or others present.
- Why the contact took place. Was it an intake interview, a routine assessment, a crisis, a counseling session?
- What took place during the contact. What did the client tell you? What behaviors did you observe? What did the client agree to do? What did you or any other professionals present agree to do?

5: Be concise.

We have discussed the importance of being concise when you are writing for people with limited literacy skills. Although the audiences for your documentation are unlikely to have limited literacy skills, individuals within or outside your agency who need to read your notes for any reason probably do have limited time. No one wants to read ten sentences when the significant points can be summarized in two sentences.

For all narrative recording, you must decide how much detail is necessary and what you can omit without compromising accuracy or completeness. Certainly, it is important to include details if a client's circumstances change significantly, if safety is an issue, if a crisis occurs, if you're concerned about liability, or if there are changes in goals or treatment (Sidell, 2011). However, it is possible to be concise *and* complete when you describe significant events and activities for the case record.

Once you begin practicing the skills required to write clearly and concisely enough for clients to understand what you write, you will find that those same skills will help you improve the clarity and conciseness of your documentation. The more you practice writing this way, the less effort it will take. Example 8.4 compares two wordy progress notes with two concise notes to demonstrate that you can omit unnecessary words without omitting crucial information.

Example 8.4   **Wordy versus Concise Notes**

Progress Note 1

Wordy	Concise
Client told me she has not had enough money to buy food when she goes shopping since she lost her job. Told me that when she feels well enough, she takes the bus to the soup kitchen for a meal. She says some days she doesn't eat and that she has lost 10 pounds in the last month. Cried when she told me she doesn't like the idea of applying for food stamps. Says it embarrasses her to ask for help but she has thought about it a lot and has will probably need food stamps in order to get by. I told her I would bring information about applying for food stamps when I visit next week. [118 words]	Client reports insufficient income to buy food since losing her job. Eats some meals at soup kitchen; sometimes skips meals. Reports losing 10 pounds in past month. Became tearful about need to "ask for help" but will consider applying for food stamps. I will bring client food stamp information next week. [51 words]

Progress Note 2

Client explained to worker that she is too sick and disabled with diabetes and heart disease to care for her elderly mother. Her mother has Alzheimer's and lives with her and is very hard to care for and needs lots of help. Worker told client she will call Home Health to see if they can help. Worker will make a referral to Home Health for an assessment of client and her mother in hopes help can be received with daily tasks and health care needs. [85 words]	Client stated she is disabled from diabetes and heart disease. Said she can no longer care for her mother who has Alzheimer's and lives with her. Worker will refer client to Home Health for assessment of home care needs. [39 words]

In exercise 8.1 you can practice identifying key information and using it to rewrite wordy notes more concisely.

Exercise 8.1   Making Wordy Notes More Concise

Note 1

Client called worker to report she had just been fired from her job. She started to cry while we were talking. She said her boss told her to pack up her things and leave immediately. She didn't even have a chance to say good bye to her co-workers. She said she had to have a job to support her children. She was so upset that worker asked her if she was thinking of hurting herself. She said she was not but that she didn't know what she was going to do to support her children. Worker made appointment for home visit tomorrow.

List the significant facts in this note:

_____

_____

Use the facts to write a more concise note:

_____

_____

_____

_____

_____

Note 2

Client and her daughter came into the office. Client said the daughter, who is 19, is pregnant. The daughter lives at home and goes to school. She had a positive pregnancy test so she really is pregnant. Client told worker that she "hates" the daughter's boyfriend because he's a "low-life." Daughter stated that she wants an abortion. Mother said that she won't allow her daughter to have an abortion. Mother said she will take the baby and raise it herself because she always wanted another baby. She told daughter that if she has an abortion, she can "just move out" of the home. Worker referred client and daughter for family counseling.

List the significant facts in this note:

_____

_____

Use the facts to write a more concise note:

_____

_____

_____

_____

_____

6: Be specific and descriptive.

Documentation that is specific and descriptive can help you monitor clients' progress—or lack of progress—toward their goals. Vague language forces anyone who reads your notes to interpret what you write. Consider some words you might use to describe a client: *sad, upset, frustrated, uneasy, happy, confused, overweight, dirty*. These words can mean different things to different people. It is far better to record what you observed and what the client or collateral contacts said. (Collateral contacts are people who have knowledge about the client with whom you communicate in person, on the phone, or in writing. They can include family members, friends, neighbors, and other professionals.) By using specific, descriptive language to document what you hear and see, you can avoid embedding unintended assessments or judgments in your documentation. If your intention is to provide an assessment, impression, or interpretation, state that clearly.

At first glance, the advice to be specific and descriptive while also being concise may appear contradictory. It does take more words to be specific and descriptive. The idea is to be specific and descriptive without using *unnecessary* words. As illustrated in example 8.5 specific, descriptive language can eliminate guesswork and make it clear what took place without being wordy.

Example 8.6 shows two vague notes that give the worker's conclusions or opinions about clients' behavior but offer no basis for those conclusions. The specific, descriptive notes document observations that provide a basis for the worker's interpretation of the situation.

Consider also the importance of specificity when you are describing how much, how many, or how often. Try to avoid using vague words such as *several, various, often, frequent, some, most, many, a lot*, and *few*. Whenever you can, be specific. For example, say how many Alcoholics Anonymous (AA) meetings the client says she attends per week or per month rather than "she states she goes to a lot of AA meetings" or "she reports she often goes to AA meetings." Instead of saying that the client "had several job interviews recently," say she "had three job interviews in the past two weeks." Reporting that your client "says she has some problems with her children" is not worth documenting unless you state what those problems are.

Example 8.5	Vague Notes versus Specific, Descriptive Notes
Vague	Concise
Client was sad and withdrawn.	Client cried several times and made no
Refused to answer worker's questions.	eye contact with worker. Answered
	worker's questions with "I don't know."

Client reports husband drinks a lot. She says when he's drunk he causes lots of trouble at home and scares the children.

Client reports husband drinks 12 beers three or four nights a week. When he drinks, he threatens to beat the children although she states he does not hit them.

Client told worker her son has problems at school and is hard to handle at home.

Client told worker her son gets in fistfights at school once or twice a week. He started a fire in his bedroom last month and strangled the family cat about six weeks ago.

Example 8.6   **Documenting the Basis for Conclusions**

Notes without Basis for Conclusions

Client got very angry with her father when he spilled a cup of coffee. She is not a good caregiver.

Notes with Basis for Conclusions

Worker observed client swear at her father and slap his hand when he spilled a cup of coffee. Worker is concerned that client may be physically abusive to her father.

Ms. Smith is a very angry woman. She is so upset about her husband leaving that she is ignoring her children's needs.

Ms. Smith stated she is "pissed off" at her husband for "walking out on us." She pounded the table and shouted he was "a son-of-a bitch." When the children began crying and pulling at her shirt, she told them to "shut up." It appears that Ms. Smith's reaction to her husband leaving may be interfering with her ability to respond appropriately to her children's needs.

Exercise 8.2   **What Does This Mean?**

The statements below could be interpreted differently by different people. As written, they do not provide useful information. Write an alternative version of each statement that is specific and descriptive:

1. The client appeared very sad. [What did the client say? What nonverbal behavior communicated sadness?]

   _____

   _____

2. Mrs. Feeble does not feed her children properly. [What did you observe that leads to this conclusion?]

   _____

   _____

3. The client was uncooperative. [What did the client communicate verbally? Nonverbally?]

   _____

   _____

4. The child told this worker his father is mean to him. [What actions or words did the child describe as "mean?"]

   _____

   _____

5. The client has no interest in leaving her abusive partner. [What did she say or do that indicated lack of interest?]

   _____

   _____

7: Be objective.

Being objective means reporting the facts "as perceived without distortion by personal feelings, prejudices, or interpretations" (*Merriam-Webster's Online Dictionary*). Complete objectivity is difficult, if not impossible, for most human beings. While you may not be able to avoid having judgmental thoughts about particular clients, their behavior, or their environments, this should not prevent you from using objective language to write your observations in progress notes, assessments, case summaries, and other documentation. A statement such as "the client is a drunk" assigns a negative label. If you write, "the client smelled of alcohol. The worker observed three empty whisky bottles on the living room floor," you are using objective language to describe what you smelled and saw. Anyone who reads that statement can draw his or her own conclusions.

As we demonstrate in example 8.7, being specific and descriptive will not only make your documentation clearer, it can also help you to be objective and avoid judgmental language. But please note that being judgmental is not the same thing as making professional judgments. It is appropriate and necessary for human service professionals to make professional judgments as they assess, intervene, and monitor clients' progress, but your professional judgments should be based on specific evidence. This means that you clearly state what you observed, where you got your information, the criteria you used to reach your conclusions, and your assessment of the situation (Kagle & Kopels, 2008). In the case of Mr. Jones, the objectively written note would provide the basis for services or referrals the worker might offer.

Example 8.7	**Changing Judgmental Language to Objective Language**
Judgmental	Objective
Mr. Jones doesn't bother to clean. His house is filthy and stinks.	Mr. Jones reports being "too tired" to clean. His floors are covered with boxes, trash, and old newspapers. The house smells of urine.

Assessments

Thus far in this chapter, we have applied the guidelines for documentation primarily to progress notes. These guidelines are equally important when you write assessments. Whether you are writing them at intake, at intervals during your work with clients, or at termination, the purpose of assessments is to "place all of the relevant information we know about a client into a concise statement that permits another professional reader to understand the client and the client's problems(s) as well as we understand them" (Glicken, 2008, p. 94). This means your assessments must clearly, specifically, and objectively describe your observations of behavior as well as what clients have communicated to you verbally and nonverbally.

While you may know exactly what you mean by labels such as "uncooperative," "uneasy," or "excitable," it is better to describe what you observed and what you were told that led to such conclusions. If you use vague language or ambiguous labels, your assessments will not allow others to understand your clients and their situations and may call into question how well you yourself understand.

COMMUNICATING WITH CLIENTS IN WRITING

We include letters and email here because copies of correspondence are part of your documentation. This is true also for text messages that are in any way significant to your work with a client. If you use email or send formal letters to communicate with clients, readability is just as important as it is in other forms of print designed for clients. Clients will benefit if they can read and understand every email or letter you send. You and your agency will benefit if the messages in the letters and emails in your case records are clear, concise, and specific.

Form Letters

In our experience, form letters are often not as clear or concise as they could be. If that is true of your agency's letters, consider revising the letters to improve their readability. In example 8.8 we have revised an excerpt from a form letter to increase readability. Figure 8.1 provides a checklist of suggestions, adapted from www.plainlanguage.gov for making letters more readable.

Example 8.8	**Making a Form Letter More Readable**
Original Letter	Revised Letter
If, due to your active military status, you will suffer a reduction of income and find it difficult to maintain your mortgage obligation, the Act provides that the interest rate of your mortgage can be reduced to 6 percent per annum until your period	Here are some things you should know before you go on active duty. If you will earn less money while on active duty, your mortgage holder can lower the interest rate on your home loan to 6 percent. You will not owe any extra interest when your

of active duty has ended. You will incur no penalty or obligation to repay the forgiven interest amount. Therefore, you should inform the holder of your mortgage (or its agent) of your inability to continue the payments required by your mortgage contract. If you have already fallen behind in your monthly payments, the holder of your loan can defer payment of the delinquent amount until your period of active duty has ended, and at that time you should make arrangements for a repayment schedule.

active duty ends. If you are behind on your home loan now, your mortgage holder can allow you to repay that money when you return from active duty.

To arrange for this, you must tell your mortgage holder that you will not be able to pay your mortgage while you are on active duty. You will also need to set up a plan for repaying the money you owe.

Figure 8.1   **Readability Checklist for Letters**

1. Begin with the main message

   Whether the main message is good news or bad news, it is what your audience needs to know, for example, whether or not they are eligible for services or that the agency is closing their case.

2. Follow the main message with any additional need-to-know information

   Additional information might include what to expect when their benefits begin, further steps they must take to initiate services, or what they can do if they were denied services or benefits.

3. Use short sections for a long letter with headings for each section

   As with other print materials we have discussed, readers can better follow the text if there are headers to introduce each topic, for example, "what you are eligible for," "how to apply for services," "what to bring to your first appointment."

4. Use personal pronouns

   Remember that a conversational style increases readability. Refer to the client as "you" rather than "applicant," "beneficiary," or "client."

5. Use active voice

   Do not hide behind passive voice, for example, "the application has been denied." Tell them in active voice, "We have denied your application."

6. Use lists.

   Rather than write "be sure to bring your pay stubs, rent receipt, income tax returns, and insurance information," you can use a list, for example:

   Be sure to bring:

   - pay stubs

   - rent receipts

   - income tax returns

   - insurance information

Email

Although we discussed general guidelines for email in chapter 6, there are additional considerations you should be aware of if you use email with clients. Just as with letters, emails should be printed or saved and retained for the case record. Be aware that because emails are part of the client's record, they can be subpoenaed or used as documentation in legal or administrative proceedings (Morgan, 2012). When you are emailing clients, you should use the same degree of formality you would use in a letter rather than the casual or informal style you might use when you email colleagues and friends. It is also worth remembering that clients can easily forward your email messages to others. Consider any potential consequences that might result if the client were to share the email.

Text Messaging

Texting is a quick way to communicate with clients to set up an appointment, let them know you're on your way to a home visit, or send them information that might interest them. Texting should be done cautiously. It is hard to avoid errors when composing a text message on a small screen, and text messages with errors may not be taken seriously. As we noted with email, remember that it is easy for the recipient to pass text messages on to others without your knowledge. You can save text messages by forwarding them to your email, and you should do so for text messages that are "clinically relevant" (Reamer, 2011). They document communications with clients and are admissible in court, thus they should be part of the case record.

A FEW FINAL WORDS

We hope you will find, as we have, that the more conscious you become of the importance of readability, the more you incorporate these principles into your professional writing. We hope, too, that we have convinced you—if you needed to be convinced—that writing clearly for clients and others is a worthwhile goal. If you already saw the need to do this, we hope the information in this book gives you the tools you need to improve the readability of all of the print and electronic materials your agency produces.

REFERENCES

Glicken, M. D. (2008). *A guide to writing for human service professionals*. Lanham, MD: Rowman & Littlefield.

Kagle, J. D., & Kopels, S. (2008). *Social work records* (3rd ed.). Long Grove, IL: Waveland.

Morgan, S. (2012). *Social workers, smartphones and electronic health information*. National Association of Social Workers, Legal Defense Fund, Legal Issue of the Month. Retrieved from https://www.social workers.org/ldf/legal_issue/2012/May2012.asp.

National Organization for Human Services. (n.d.). *Ethical standards for human service professionals*. Retrieved from http://www.national humanservices.org/ethical-standards-for-hs-professionals#clients.

Reamer, F. G. (2005). Documentation in social work: Evolving ethical and risk-management standards. *Social Work, 50*, 325–334. doi: 10.1093/sw/50.4.325.

Reamer, F. G. (2011). Developing a social media ethics policy. *Social Work Today.* Retrieved from http://www.socialworktoday.com/news/eoe_070111.shtml.

Sidell, N. L. (2011). *Social work documentation*. Washington, DC: NASW Press.

Souders, T., Strom-Gottfried, K., & DeVito, D. (2011). FAQ on documentation and clinical records. *Theiman Advisory*. School of Social Work, University of North Carolina at Chapel Hill.

Wilson, S. J. (1980). *Recording: Guidelines for social workers*. New York: Free Press.

A Brief Review of Grammar and Punctuation

This is not a comprehensive guide to perfect grammar and punctuation. In fact, we're not sure perfect grammar and punctuation are achievable because there are, among grammarians, some hotly contested differences of opinion. We recognize that rules for correct usage can be complicated and difficult to remember. However, correct grammar, punctuation, and spelling are important for clarity, and that makes them important elements of readability. Our intent is to provide sound advice on grammar and punctuation basics without overwhelming you. The material included here should help you avoid a number of common writing errors. No matter what kind of professional writing you do, you will come across as more credible if your writing is free of common grammatical and punctuation errors.

If you are a human service practitioner, you have to learn to navigate gray areas in your day-to-day work. And so it is with the rules that govern writing, where there are also gray areas. If you were paying close attention to the writing conventions—for example, capitalization and punctuation—in this book, you will notice some differences between the rules we describe here and the style used throughout the book. There is an explanation for these differences. The guidelines we recommend below for grammar and punctuation are based on the *Publication Manual of the American Psychological Association* (often referred to as APA style). APA rules govern the style we use for formal writing in the social sciences. Lyceum Books, the publisher of this book, follows the style rules in *The Chicago Manual of Style*.

GRAMMAR BASICS

The dictionary defines grammar as "(a) the study of the classes of words, their inflections, and their functions and relations in the sentence [and] (b) a study of what is to be preferred and what avoided in inflection and syntax" (*Merriam-Webster's Online Dictionary*). Our own simple definition is that grammar is the accepted set of rules for using the language. How well you know and follow those rules is not a measure of how smart you are, how much you know, or how competent you are professionally, but obvious and frequent grammatical, punctuation, and spelling errors are distracting for readers. They may convey a lack of competence or inattention to detail particularly to those who know you only by what you write. If your purpose is to communicate clear messages to clients and others, be aware that grammar, punctuation, and spelling are integral to clarity.

We all learned certain habits of speech as children. If you grew up hearing and speaking standard English, and especially if you read a lot as a child, you probably do not give much thought to grammar. If you grew up among people who did not speak standard English, or who spoke a language other than English, using "correct" grammar may not come easily for you. To make things even more complicated, the rules for using language evolve and change over time. Despite this, there are some areas that cause problems even for many educated people. We will review these with an eye to those areas that are especially important for professional writing.

Spelling
The small amount of time it takes to look up a word online or in a dictionary can save you the embarrassment of publicly displaying misspellings for others to read. Your computer's spell-check function can also help you spot errors, but it is no substitute for proofreading. It will not catch common typographical errors or misused words, as this sentence illustrates:

> It's the *plane* truth, and a *reel* shame, but you must *except* that a spell-checker will not pick up words that you spell correctly but *ewes* incorrectly.

Capitalization

Determining when and what to capitalize can be confusing. It's easy to remember to capitalize the first word in a sentence or the names of people, cities, and countries because these words are always capitalized. As we will discuss shortly, there are words that are capitalized in some circumstances but not in others. Before we get to those, let's review the basic rules for capitalization.

- Capitalize the first word in a complete sentence that follows a colon.

  The agency director announced the following: All employees will be required to use their vacation days as soon as possible.

- Capitalize the first word in a quotation within a sentence.

  The client told me, "Get lost."

- Capitalize the names of specific places, things, organizations, businesses, and government agencies.

  She is originally from Connecticut. She used to work for the Department of Veterans' Affairs and currently owns Dickie's Doggy Daycare.

- Capitalize letters that stand for words.

  He belongs to NASW (National Association of Social Workers).

- Capitalize a title that comes before a name.

  Executive Director Sara Bellum has announced her retirement.

- Capitalize trade and brand names.

  The client takes Tylenol for her headaches.

- Capitalize deities.

  Her friend taught her about similarities in the teachings of Jesus and Buddha.

- Capitalize religions.

  His family is quite diverse and includes Muslims, Christians, and Jews.

- Capitalize racial designations

  The intake form asks applicants to identify as Black, White, Hispanic, Asian, or Native American.

- Capitalize languages.

  We are looking for a Spanish-speaking social worker.

- Capitalize nationalities.

  Our agency serves Mexican, Russian, Chinese, and African immigrants.

- Do not capitalize the seasons: spring, summer, fall, winter.

We wish we could tell you that the rules for capitalization are as easy as always capitalizing some words and never capitalizing others. Alas, the rules are much more complicated than that. So now for the hard part—words that are capitalized in some circumstances but not in others.

- Do not capitalize words like *north, south, east* and *west* when you are using them as a direction or as part of a description.

  Our office is a block south of the intersection.

- Do capitalize *north, south, east* and *west* when they are part of a place or organization name or when they denote a geographic region.

  Because his health condition worsens in cold weather, he moved to the South last year.

- Do not capitalize common nouns. Common nouns denote general categories rather than specific people, places, or things. One way to recognize a common noun is that it may be preceded by an article such as *a, an,* or *the.*

  The board elected a new president. [In this sentence *president* is a common noun and is not capitalized.]

- Do capitalize a noun that represents a specific person, place, or thing.

  The board meeting was called to order by President Lynn Gweeny. [In this sentence *president* is a title and should be capitalized.]

Subject-Verb Agreement

A singular subject requires a singular verb; a plural subject requires a plural verb. This presents little difficulty in simple sentences. However, in some sentences it can be difficult to identify the subject, which makes it hard to decide whether to use a singular or plural verb. It is especially problematic when there are several words between the subject of the sentence and the verb. If you are not sure which word is the subject, you may find it helpful to mentally remove any words that describe or modify the subject. The sentence will still make sense without these modifiers.

A person with limited literacy skills is at a disadvantage.

The subject is *person* and it is singular. The words *with limited literacy skills* tell you something about the subject but do not change the fact that the subject is singular. You would use the singular verb *is*.

Increases in insurance coverage have improved the community's overall health.

In this sentence, the subject is *increases*, which is plural. The words *in insurance coverage* provide information about the subject. The plural subject requires the plural verb *have*.

Whether to use a singular or plural verb can also be confusing when a prepositional phrase such as *in addition to* or *as well as* comes between the subject and the verb. Removing those phrases will help you identify the subject.

Poverty, as well as educational attainment, is a significant factor in literacy.

The phrase *as well as* does not change the fact that the subject of the sentence is the word *poverty*, which is singular.

One final area of potential difficulty is when subjects are joined by words *or* or *nor*. The rule here is that the subject closest to the verb is the one that must agree with the verb.

Neither the children nor the father *is* willing to discuss the incident.

Children and *father* make up the compound subject in this sentence. The verb *is* must agree with the second part of the subject—*father*—which is singular.

The father or the children *are* going to explain what happened.

In this sentence, the verb *are* is plural because the plural part of the subject—*children*—is closest to it.

In exercise A.1 you can practice matching subjects and verbs in sentences where modifiers appear between the subject and the verb.

Exercise A.1 **Subject-Verb Agreement**

1. The director, *as well as* members of the board, [___ is ___ are] responsible for approving job descriptions.

2. The new contracts, *in addition to* a recent grant, [___ allow ___ allows] us to expand our programming.

3. An individual who has no job skills [___ is ___ are] at a disadvantage in the job market.

4. Family members or a pastor [___ is ___ are] encouraged to visit.

5. Neither a family member nor friends [___ is ___ are] allowed to sit in on the assessment.

6. Workers, in collaboration with the client, [___ develop ___ develops] treatment goals.

7. A staff member or volunteers [___ remain ___ remains] in the room at all times.

8. Regular program reviews, conducted by an outside auditor, [___ contribute ___ contributes] to agency productivity.

Exercise A.1 Answer Key

1. *Is* because it agrees with the singular subject *director*.

2. *Allows* because it refers to the singular subject *contract*.

3. *Is* because it agrees with the singular subject *individual*.

4. *Is* because it agrees with *pastor* which is the second subject.

5. *Are* because it agrees with *friend*s which is the second subject.

6. *Develop* because it agrees with the plural subject *workers*.

7. *Remain* because it agrees with the second subject *volunteers*.

8. *Contribute* because it agrees with the plural subject *reviews*.

Pronoun Agreement

Pronouns can replace nouns and other pronouns, but when you use a pronoun to replace a noun or another pronoun, you must be sure they agree. This means that both words should be either singular or plural.

Correct:

The parents [*plural noun*] were escorted to their [*plural pronoun*] child's classroom.

The counselor [*singular noun*] sees each of her [*singular pronoun*] clients for 45 minutes a week.

Incorrect:

The mother [*singular noun*] was escorted to their [*plural pronoun*] child's classroom.

Collective nouns such as *agency, committee, board of directors, team, group*, and *staff* can be confusing because they are single units made up of more than one person. This can make them seem plural when they are, in fact, singular. One way to determine if a noun is singular or plural is to add an "s." If you can make it plural by adding an "s," it is singular without the "s." This technique will help you avoid the common mistake of using the plural pronouns *they* or *theirs* when referring to a collective noun.

Correct:

The *team* elected *its* leader.

The *teams* elected *their* leaders.

Incorrect:

The *team* elected *their* leader.

Correct:

The *group* had *its* final session on Friday.

The *groups* had *their* final session on Friday.

Incorrect:

The *group* had *their* final session on Friday.

Another area that can be difficult is deciding whether to use a singular or plural pronoun to replace an indefinite pronoun such as *someone, anyone, each, everybody, no one, something, either.* Indefinite pronouns are similar to collective nouns. They may appear to refer to more than one, and thus be plural, but they are actually considered singular.

Correct:

Each works with a counselor to develop *his or her* treatment plan.

Incorrect:

Each works with a counselor to develop *their* treatment plan.

Correct:

Because of the proposed budget cuts, everyone is uneasy about *his or her* job.

Incorrect:

Because of the proposed budget cuts, everyone is uneasy about *their* job.

Exercise A.2 challenges you apply what we've just discussed to identify the correct pronouns in each sentence.

Exercise A.2	Noun-Pronoun Agreement

1. When beginning a new job, it is common for an employee to worry about [___his or her ___ their] performance.
2. The committee prepared an announcement and [___ it ___ they] emailed it to all staff before the meeting.
3. The members of the board signed [___its ___ their] names to the letter requesting the director's resignation.

4. If one of the group members acts out, call me, and I'll talk to [___ him or her ___ them].

5. When someone smokes in the shelter, [___ he or she ___ they] are asked to leave.

6. When there is a board of directors, [___ it ___ they] will be responsible for financial oversight.

7. Neither the mother nor the siblings offered [___ his or her ___ their] opinion about the child's behavior.

8. One of the administrators will lose [___ his or her ___ their] position.

Exercise A.2 Answer Key

1. *His or her* because it refers to the singular noun *employee*.
2. *It* because it refers to the collective noun *committee*.
3. *Their* because it refers to the plural *members*.
4. *Him or her* because it refers to the singular *one*.
5. *He or she* t because *someone* refers to one person.
6. *It* because it refers to the collective noun *board of directors*.
7. *Their* because it refers to the plural *siblings* which comes after *nor*.
8. *His or her* because it refers to the noun *one*.

Avoiding Sexist Pronoun Use

You may have noticed that we replaced singular nouns with the pronoun phrase "his or her." We recognize that it would be less awkward to say, "Each client works with a counselor to develop *his* treatment plan." However, we believe it is important for human service professionals to avoid using sexist language. Using the generic *he* or *his* to represent all clients is considered sexist and is therefore unacceptable. Fortunately, you can often avoid the awkwardness of using "his or her" by using the plural.

Singular:

Each client works with a counselor to develop *his or her* treatment plan.

Plural:

All clients work with a counselor to develop *their* treatment plans.

Singular:

A worker must update *his or her* client assessments every six months.

Plural:

Workers must update *their* client assessments every six months.

Pronoun Case

Case is the form of a pronoun that shows its relationship to other words in a sentence. There are three cases: subjective, objective, and possessive. Because you are not likely to misuse possessive pronouns (*my, mine, your, yours, his, her, hers, its, our, ours, their, theirs*, and *whose*), we will focus on subjective and objective pronouns. They are, unfortunately, often abused, confused, and misused even by highly educated people.

Subjective pronouns, as the name suggests, can be the subject of either independent or dependent clauses. They include: *I, you, he, she, it, we, they*, and *who*. Few people are likely to use a subjective pronoun incorrectly when it is the subject of an independent or dependent clause.

Independent clause:

We will be in the office to take applications.

Dependent clause:

we who work in the office

Other uses of subjective pronouns can be problematic. You should use a subjective pronoun after any form of the verb *to be*.

Correct:

It is *I* who will complete your evaluation.

Incorrect:

It is *me* who will complete your evaluation.

Objective pronouns act as the objects or recipients of an action. They include: *me, you, him, her, it, us, them*, and *whom*. They present no difficulty when used as follows:

Direct objects:

My supervisor gave *me* an excellent evaluation.

The objects of prepositions:

George prepared the report for *us*.

Indirect objects:

Samantha provided *him* with valuable information.

The subjects of infinitives:

We require *them* to bring proof of eligibility.

The most frequent pronoun case errors we observe are in sentences that contain a compound joined by *and, but,* or *or.* It may only be grammar geeks (like us) who are aware of these errors. These misuses of pronoun case are so common, in speech and in writing, that the correct usage may appear incorrect.

Correct:

They gave Maisie and *me* a logical explanation.

They will allow Moe or *me* to attend the conference.

Incorrect:

They gave Maisie and *I* a logical explanation.

They will allow Moe or *I* to attend the conference.

There is an easy way to choose the correct pronoun for sentences with compound subjects or objects. Just ask yourself which pronoun you would use if you removed the initial noun or pronoun. In the example above, if you take out the words *Maisie* and *Moe*, you can easily see that it would be incorrect to say "They gave *I* a logical explanation" or "They will allow *I* to attend the conference." Instead you would use the correct pronoun, which is *me*. If you remember this trick of mentally removing the initial noun or pronoun, you can avoid making this very common mistake.

One last area of pronoun confusion is choosing the correct pronoun when you are making a comparison. In comparison sentences, you will usually see the words *than* or *as* before the comparison.

Correct:

My colleague is paid better than *I.*

She works the same number of hours as *I.*

Incorrect:

My colleague is paid better than *me.*

She works the same number of hours as *me.*

A comparison usually leaves out a word or words. Mentally filling in the missing word or words will help you decide which pronoun is correct. In the example above you could say "My colleague is paid better than *I am paid*" or "She works the same number of hours as *I work*." You would not say "My colleague is paid better than *me is paid*." Nor would you say "She works the same number of hours as *me work*." Exercise A.3 will give you practice using the correct pronoun case.

Exercise A.3	Pronoun Case: An Exercise for You and Me

1. My supervisor and [___I ___me] will attend the meeting.
2. The training program was developed just for [___we ___us] employees.
3. [___We ___Us] human service professionals are sometimes under-appreciated.
4. My co-workers are a lot more relaxed about the grant than [___I ___me].
5. The director asked [___she ___her] and [___I ___me] to write a grant.
6. They told the police officer and [___I ___me] it was a mistake.
7. We are fortunate to have a manager as experienced as [___he ___him].
8. It was [___they ___them] who were supposed to do the paperwork.

Exercise A.3 Pronoun Case Answer Key

1. *I.* You would not say "*me* will attend."
2. *us.* You would not say "developed just for *we.*"
3. *We.* You would not say "*us* are sometimes underappreciated."
4. *I.* You would not say "than *me* am relaxed."
5. *her* and *me.* You would not say "asked *she*" or "asked *I.*"
6. *me.* You would not say "told *I* it was a mistake."
7. *he.* You would not say "as experienced as *him* is."
8. *they.* You would not say "*them* were supposed to do the paperwork."

Sentences

A complete sentence, also known as an independent clause, has a subject and a verb and expresses a complete thought.

Complete sentence:

The community gathered to mourn the loss of a respected leader.

A sentence fragment or incomplete sentence is also called a dependent clause. It may have a subject and a verb but does not express a complete thought.

When the community gathered to mourn the loss of a respected leader. [This thought is incomplete. It doesn't tell us what happened when the community gathered.]

You can join two independent clauses—or two complete sentences— with a coordinating conjunction such as *and, but, or, nor, so,* or *yet* to form a compound sentence. To do this correctly, you must insert a comma before the conjunction.

The agency is seeking input from consumers, *and* it will hold several community forums.

You can also use a semicolon to combine two independent clauses into one compound sentence.

The agency is seeking input from consumers; it will hold several community forums.

A run-on sentence incorrectly combines two complete sentences into one. There are two types of run-on sentences: two sentences that are joined without any punctuation and two sentences joined with a comma but no conjunction, called a comma splice.

Two sentences, no punctuation:

The agency serves low income women it offers a variety of services.

Comma splice:

The agency serves low income women, it offers a variety of services.

There are two ways to correct these run-on sentences. You can separate the two independent clauses with a semicolon or you can insert a coordinating conjunction preceded by a comma.

Adding a semicolon:

The agency serves low income women; it offers a variety of services.

Adding a conjunction:

The agency serves low income women, and it offers a variety of services.

PUNCTUATION BASICS

At first glance, you might think punctuation is a relatively minor issue. It is true that some readers may not notice misplaced commas or apostrophes, but punctuation matters. As we illustrate in example A.1, you can change meaning by changing punctuation. No doubt the fictional Ms. Wonk would be pleased to get the first letter. She would be much less pleased if she were to receive the second letter.

| Example A.1 | Punctuation in a Letter |

Dear Ms. Wonk:

We value employees who understand what hard work is all about. You are motivated, competent and smart. Staff members who are different from you acknowledge being unprofessional and careless. Your performance standards have been a disaster for other staff members. Who will be qualified to take your place and maintain high standards after you leave? We are very grateful.

Dear Ms. Wonk:

We value employees who understand what hard work is. All about you are motivated, competent and staff members who are different from you. Acknowledge being unprofessional and careless. Your performance standards have been a disaster. For other staff members who will be qualified to take your place and maintain high standards after you leave, we are very grateful.

The words in the letters are identical. The only difference between them is the punctuation. It is the punctuation, of course, that completely changes the meaning, demonstrating just how critical punctuation is. Although punctuation is only one element of clarity, it helps to ensure that what you write conveys the meaning you intend. We stress throughout this book the importance of using plain language and writing simply and clearly. The more simply and clearly you write, the less punctuation you will need. Even so, knowing what and how to punctuate is not always as easy as we might wish.

Commas

Some writers use too many commas, and some use too few. Our goal is to help you punctuate your writing with the right number of commas. Just because you can insert a comma does not mean you should. The only time to use a comma is when you know you need one. How do you know if you need one? That question is the subject of hot debate. Regarding the Oxford or serial comma, for example: both sides agree that three or more items in a list should be separated by commas. The disagreement is over whether to insert a comma before the coordinating conjunction (e.g., *and* or *or*) at the end of the list: "The agency offers assessment, referrals, education, and counseling." That final comma is called the Oxford or serial comma, and many favor dropping it: "The agency offers assessment, referrals, education and counseling." We prefer using a comma before a conjunction because we believe it increases clarity. Whatever your choice, do remember to be consistent in using or not using the serial comma

Other uses of the comma are not so contentious. Use a comma when you list a series of adjectives in any place it would be appropriate to insert the word *and*.

> Most of our clients are poor, young, single women. [You could also write: The clients are poor *and* young *and* single women.]

Enclose parenthetical words or expressions between commas. A parenthetical word or expression is a word or phrase you can remove and still have a complete sentence.

> Our program, which serves low-income children, is free to eligible families. [The sentence would be complete and make sense if you wrote: Our program is free to eligible families.]

Use commas to set off abbreviations such as *etc.*, *i.e.*, and *e.g.*, the abbreviations for academic degrees, and titles that follow a name.

We provide toiletries such as shampoo, soap, etc., to the residents.

Ray Bann, MSW, is president of our board of directors.

Anna Banana, an influential community member, has expressed strong support for our program.

Use a comma between the day of the month and the year and one after the year for a specific date. Do not use any commas when you write the month and year without a specific date.

We must receive proof of residence by Tuesday, April 30, 2014, to verify your eligibility for services.

We must receive proof of residence by the end of April 2014 to verify your eligibility for services.

Use a comma before the conjunctions *and, but, for, or, nor, so,* and *yet* when they are used to join two complete sentences.

Human service workers sometimes feel overworked and underpaid, but this work has intangible rewards.

Use a comma when you begin a sentence with a dependent clause. A dependent clause begins with conjunctions such as *because, although, when, before, unless,* and *as soon as.* A dependent clause cannot stand alone as a complete sentence.

Because we have a contract with the county, our fees are reasonable. [Note that if this sentence were written with the dependent clause at the end, you would *not* use a comma to separate the clauses.]

Use a comma after a word or phrase such as *however, at this time,* or *initially* that introduces the rest of a sentence.

Currently, we do not know what next year's budget will cover. *In the meantime*, we will carry on as best we can.

Whenever you are tempted to add a comma to your writing, ask yourself why you need one. If you cannot think of a rule that says you need a comma, leave it out.

Apostrophes

As with commas, people often insert apostrophes where they do not belong and omit them when they should be used. We have tried to summarize here what you need to know about the apostrophe.

Before the *s* to indicate the possessive of a singular noun:

The *agency's* waiting room is being renovated.

After the *s* to indicate the possessive of a plural noun that ends in *s*:

The *clients'* records are electronically stored.

To form the plural of numbers and lower case letters:

6's and 7's; p's and q's

To form a contraction:

She's [she is] going to apply for a job. She *doesn't* [does not] have a car, and *it's* [it has] been difficult for her to find employment.

Note (please, please note!) that you need an apostrophe when you use *it's* as a contraction of *it is* or *it has*. That is the only correct use of *it's*. One very common mistake is to use *it's* in place of the possessive pronoun *its*. You can avoid this mistake by reading the sentence to yourself and substituting *it is* or *it has* for the contraction. If the substitution works, you need the apostrophe; if it doesn't work, remove the apostrophe because you are using the possessive pronoun.

It's important to note that the organization received *its* first grant this year.

It is as important to avoid unnecessary apostrophes as it is to insert apostrophes where they belong.

- Do not add apostrophes to the possessive pronouns *hers, his, yours, ours, theirs,* and *whose.*

- Do not use apostrophes to form the plural of acronyms, abbreviations, or dates.
- Never, never, never use an apostrophe to form the plural of a word.

There is debate among the experts about whether to add an apostrophe *s* to proper nouns that end in *s* to form the possessive. The classic *Elements of Style* by Strunk and White and the *Oxford Dictionary* advocate adding apostrophe *s* to nouns ending in *s* when you would naturally pronounce the *s* if you said the word out loud (e.g., the *boss's* book). These sources also suggest adding apostrophe *s* to names that end in *s* (e.g., Ms. *Jones's* application). On the other side of the debate, the *U. S. Government Printing Office Style Manual* (http://www.gpo.gov/fdsys/search/pagedetails.action?granuleId=&packageId=GPO-STYLEMANUAL-2008&fromBrowse=true) and the *Chicago Manual of Style*, 16th edition, which is most often used in book publishing, advise eliminating the extra *s* (e.g., the *boss'* book; Ms. *Jones'* application). You can choose the approach you prefer, but whatever you decide, be sure to do it consistently.

PARALLEL CONSTRUCTION

Parallel construction (sometimes called parallel structure) means using the same pattern of words or phrases in a sentence or list. In addition to being correct usage, parallel construction gives your writing consistency, and consistency makes it clearer and improves readability. To achieve parallel construction, avoid combining –ing forms of verbs with infinitive forms and be consistent in wording phrases within a sentence.

Not parallel:

The client's two goals are *to learn* to read and *completing* her GED.

Parallel:

The client's two goals are *learning* to read and *completing* her GED.

The client's two goals are *to learn* to read and *to complete* her GED.

Not parallel:

We ask applicants to provide proof of residence, that they arrive on time, and bringing a utility bill.

Parallel:

We ask applicants to provide proof of residence, to arrive on time, and to bring a utility bill.

Parallel construction is important when you present a list after a colon. You can use complete sentences or fragments, but be sure you do not combine complete sentences with fragments.

Not parallel:

The program serves children:

- Who are developmentally delayed
- Diagnosed with physical disabilities
- Needing opportunities to interact with other children

Parallel:

The program serves children:

- Who have developmental delays
- Who are diagnosed with multiple disabilities
- Who need opportunities to interact with other children

Not parallel:

Our team has accomplished the following goals:

- Community member recruitment
- Developing program goals
- We wrote and submitted a small grant proposal

Parallel:

Our team has accomplished the following goals:

- Recruiting community members
- Developing program protocols
- Writing and submitting a small grant proposal

We hope you will use the information we've provided as a reference and that you will return to it as needed. We have listed a few additional references that you may find helpful.

- For finding synonyms and antonyms: http://thesaurus.com/

- For grammar, punctuation, and much more: Purdue Online Writing Lab. http://owl.english.purdue.edu/owl/resource/560/01/

- For additional grammar, punctuation, and style tips: http://www .dianahacker.com/bedhandbook6e/subpages/language.html

- For punctuation and a good laugh: L. Truss, *Eats, Shoots & Leaves: The Zero Tolerance Approach to Punctuation* (New York: Gotham Books, 2003).

- For a classic reference on grammar, punctuation, and style: W. Strunk Jr. and E. B. White, *The Elements of Style* (New York: Macmillan). Available free online at http://www.bartleby.com/141/

Index

About the Authors

Natalie Ames is associate professor in the Department of Social Work at North Carolina State University. Prior to her academic career, her social work experience included public welfare, medical social work, and individual and group counseling with survivors of sexual assault and domestic violence, as well as program development and administration, public education, and community outreach. She has developed educational materials and training programs for professionals and the general public on a wide range of topics including nutrition, smokeless tobacco, domestic violence, how to write easy-to-read materials, and social work documentation. She has written a variety of easy-to-read fact sheets and brochures for the National Cancer Institute and the Mary Babb Randolph Cancer Center at West Virginia University and has presented numerous workshops to national, regional, and statewide audiences on how to write for people with limited literacy skills.

Katy FitzGerald is a licensed clinical social worker at an inpatient psychiatric and substance abuse hospital in North Carolina. Before becoming a social worker, she spent twenty years in technology marketing, where she translated complex technology information into language nontechnical people could understand. She has a BA in communications from William Jewell College in Liberty, Missouri, and earned her MSW at North Carolina State University. She is a volunteer and former president of the board of directors of Haven House Services, a nonprofit agency in Raleigh, North Carolina, dedicated to providing services to at-risk and homeless youth.